12.8.97

Beside the Sleeping Maiden

Poets *of* Marin

Edited by
CB Follett

Arctos Press, Sausalito California

HoBear Publications

ARCTOS PRESS
P.O. Box 401
Sausalito, CA 94966-401

Cover Art: "The Oyster Road," a pastel by Joyce Livingston
Book Design: Christi Payne Fryday & CB Follett
Typography: Christi Payne Fryday, Book Arts

Library of Congress Cataloging-in-Publication Data
Follett, CB
    Beside The Sleeping Maiden : Poets of Marin / edited by CB Follett – First Edition

    ISBN 0-9657015-3-0
    1. Poetry   2. Marin County 3. California

Library of Congress Catalog Card Number: 97-71252

ACKNOWLEDGMENTS

Excerpt from *Journey to Mount Tamalpais* by Etel Adnan—*Post-Apollo Press*

"Every Day" by Ellery Akers—*Barnabe Mountain Review*

"Strawberry Fields" by Karla Andersdatter—*The Broken String,* Plain View Press 1994

"Musings" by Evelyn Belvin—*In No Particular Order* 1993

"Coming Home" by Karen Benke—*Tea Talk Quarterly*

"Two Heart Clan" by Duane BigEagle—*On the Bus*

"A Roomy Place" by Patricia Cannon—*The 33 Review VII*

"We Don't Have to Share a Fate" by Gillian Conoley—*The Missouri Review* and *Beckon,*
    Carnegie Mellon University Press 1996

"Priority Mail for My Sons" by Ruth Daigon—*Between One Future and the Next* Papier-
    Mache Press 1995

"Spain: Flamenco" by Dolores de Léon—*Stones and Amulets* 1996

"After a Certain Age a Woman Becomes Invisible" by Ella Eytan—*The Bay Guardian*

"Home" by Molly Fisk—Stinson Beach and Bolinas Libraries, National Poetry Month: 1996

"The Beekeeper's Beard" by Gerald Fleming—*Five Fingers Review*

"Bull Kelp" by CB Follett—*Confluence* and *The WindRoom Series*—Radiolarian Press

"The Roly Poly Bug" by Terri Glass—*Unveiling the Mystical Light* 1991

"Marks Which Darken or Let in Light" by Dale Going—*Rooms*

"Fishing in the Keep of Silence" copyright 1994 by Linda Gregg. Reprinted from *Chosen by
    the Lion* with the permission of Graywolf Press, Saint Paul, Minnesota

"A Story About the Body" by Robert Hass—Ecco Press 1989

"Mighty Forms" by Brenda Hillman—*Zyzzyva, Pushcart Prize XVI, 100 Great Poems by
    Women,* Ecco Press, and *Bright Existence,* Wesleyan University Press 1993

"The Love of Aged Horses" by Jane Hirshfield—*The Atlantic Monthly* and *The October
    Palace,* Harper Collins 1994

"Nine Generations Lost" by Sarah Howard—*In the House of All Strangers*

"In Memorium" by Joanne Kyger—*New Censorship*

"Engkanto" by Jaime Jacinto—*Heaven is Just Another Country* 1996

"Uncharted Flight" by Robin Heerens Lysne—*Krone* 1996, Women Poets and Writers

"Hatted" by Diane Lutovich—*Staple*

"Astrolabe" by Rosalie Moore—*Peregrine*

"Surprises" by Gerald Nicosia—*Connections* (London)

"Living on the Earthquake Fault" by Diana O'Hehir—*Power to Change Geography*

"The Death of Six Million" by Caitlin Patler—*Marin Independent Journal*

"Evening Poem (for Carolyn Kizer)" by Robert Peterson—*Leaving Taos,* Harper & Row 1981

"Sea Experience" by Jean Pumphrey—*Sheltered at the Edge* 1982

"11" by Stephen Ratcliffe—*Sculpture,* Littoral Books 1996

"Grapes" by Stefano Resta—*fish bird stone star*

"Why Animals Dance" by Kay Ryan—*Anima* and *Dragon Acts to Dragon Ends*

"Crop Circles" by Anne Bacon Soulé—*Midwest Poetry Review*

"Late October" by Linda Strauss—*# Nine,* Linda Tu Publications 1990

"Those Mornings, Big Sur" by Stephan Torre—*Man Living on a Side Creek,* New York
    University Press 1994

"The Nursery" by Laurel Trivelpiece—*Witness* and *Best Poems of 1995,* Scribners

"Crimson Tide" by Janie von Waldburg—*MC Echoes, Texas Young Writers Newsletter,
    Stone Soup*

"The Song Mt. Tamalpais Sings" by Lew Welch—*The Song Mt. Tamalpais Sings,* Sand Dollar
    1970, with permission from the estate of Lew Welch

"Invisible People" Marin Country Day School 7th Grade—*Marin Independent Journal*

"We Remember"—*Marin County Juvenile Hall Anthology*

TABLE OF CONTENTS

Once I was asked in front of a television camera: *Who is the most important person you ever met?* and I remember answering: *A mountain.* I thus discovered that Tamalpais was at the very center of my being.

I've been hiking Marin trails since I taught bird-watching here twenty years ago and banded birds at the Point Reyes Bird Observatory. The Spanish have a word for a place one feels a longing for. I have *querencia* for Point Reyes.

It's impossible to stay *out of love* / when your dreams reside / beside The Sleeping Maiden.

Being surrounded by such natural beauty in a landscape where I had no roots or history, Marin has often seemed more of a vacation in paradise than a home. Daily, I've had to work at grounding myself and making connections. Sometimes it's felt like travel, but even when I leave to travel again, this is where I'll tell people I'm from. This is where I'll always return.

I moved to Marin about six years ago. I feel a separateness as well as curiosity. Being from the East, I feel a little "outside" the landscape; the beauty of this place has some strangeness to it.

A chance reading of the College of Marin Bulletin revealed the name of Rosalie Moore Brown, sent me back to school, and provided me with fine inspiration. I organized my pile of doodles and went on and on. I miss the poetry beat and remain disabled—no fun.

Marin affects my writing in the way silence moves around me late at night. Living and sleeping so close to Mt. Tamalpais has also changed the ways in which I dream. Silence and dreams influence my writing enormously.

As an American Indian youth, I was taught to value a connection with the land, which sustains our lives. I learned early that individuality, creativity, self-expression and love of beauty are essential to the survival for a whole and healthy person. I experienced the roles that art and poetry play in the passing of culture from one generation to another.

CONTENTS

CONTENTS

CONTENTS

I came to Marin twenty years ago with the thought I would return to Washington D.C. in two years. I never looked back. I am passionately in love with the Marin landscape. I was a painter years ago, how could I not love this place. Everywhere I turn is a landscape, everywhere I turn is a poem, I need only pay attention.

I write, drawing upon my long life experience with people, birth, death, small daily wonders and the extraordinary surround of nature.

I was a child in Marin's landscape, and I can't forget it. The shapes of live oaks against pale hills. Sourgrass and lupine. What it's like looking up from downtown Mill Valley into the huge trunks of the redwoods. How straight they are; how cold the air gets underneath their branches; burst of scent from their tiny cones.

Marin? A matter of absorption, really, a *wicking* of the bioregion that holds us. One hopes to remain open, and if open, focused/not overwhelmed. So many would die for such problems, friend! In this place of conspicuous consumption, the real wealth: under our feet. Developers are salivating for it, their dried saliva like slug tracks across the trunks of rotten trees.

Poetry is all the senses, rhythm, music, and the soul. This is also what Marin means to me. It's my joy to combine them.

A sense of place is very important for me in my writing, and Marin is sinking into my bones. I can't say I will always stay here, but I will always carry a feel of these hills of grass in morning light, the smell of fennel, and fingers of fog caught in the valleys.

Marin County with its ideal temperatures and beautiful beaches seems like paradise to me and makes it more difficult to stay inside and write.

Marin is its proximities, the step outside one's door so easily leading. (I cultivate a landscape of small rectangles and plots—punctuated, blurred and defined by greenery). Each day, water alters and a density of light. Each day, I am part of the weather and the whether.

CONTENTS

CONTENTS

CONTENTS

I have hiked most of the trails on Mt. Tam and in West Marin, and it is reflected often in my poetry and painting. Even when living elsewhere it was necessary to have an occasional "Marin Fix."

I am blessed by sundry gods to care-take one small triangle of paradise in West Marin where, from season to season, I clock coho and steelhead in the backyard stream; where when no one is interfering I labor with ever-humbling results over the latest poem-in-progress, singing to myself the silliest tune.

I, along with so many others writers, have been struck by the strange almost golden light that says over and over again, "You are lucky to be living here, to enjoy a beauty that covers everything with its own glow."

In my poems appear images from the hills, Bolinas Lagoon, Point Reyes National Seashore and many other places that are dear to my heart. Marin has supported me in my independence and emergence as an unique individual.

I watched a crow bother every creature he could. The trickster's antics revived and renewed me. I am at the point where I could live anywhere I choose. There is no choice.

This poem was written while looking out my window at a sturdy narcissus during a heavy Spring downpour.

I like the trees here, and the ocean never seems too far away.

(The Astrolabe is a medieval instrument for determining the height of celestial objects.) I like to write about the convergence of visions from disparate times and cultures. But Marin is a good place from which to view them!

Marinating in Marin / Forty One Savory Years / Mellows One's Muse.

Marin is my home, for the rest of my life, I hope. It is a state of mind for me, and a peace inside my heart.

CONTENTS

CONTENTS

CONTENTS

I have probably wanted to live in Marin for some time, mostly, I think, because nature is so evident and respected here. Happily, we live among some very old trees where there is a strong sense of connection to the earth, an influence I welcome—for us, our children and our poetry.

Upon receiving notice of acceptance, I bumpt into an old Hamilton bud at the San Rafael bus station. I explained the gig, *Beside the Sleeping Maiden* and he nodded, then shook his head, saying "Better not wake her."

And Introducing . . .
Marin's Younger Poets

Mt. Tamalpais, the Cascade and Tennessee Valleys, the beaches, the stately redwood trees and brilliant colored poppies bring me peace and inspiration in my poetry, drawing and painting. Writing has been an important path of self expression for me; and I marvel at how each person has different ways of expressing themselves, and especially that poets become famous for it.

Growing up in beautiful Mill Valley, where the schools offer poetry classes to students of all grade levels, I was always encouraged to write. I was exposed to the power of poetry early and felt constant support as my writing matured.

I have lived beneath Mt. Tamalpais for most of my 14 years. My mother chose our home because it sat on a spur of the mountain and deer slept in our backyard under the apple tree. From this point, I look out into the world and have begun to see how fortunate we are. I wish everyone could live in or visit the beauty of this place, a beauty that lightens suffering. This is what poetry can do—care for others.

Living in Marin I appreciate the beauty of the natural world. However, many times it is not the presence of this beauty but the absence that opens my eyes widest.

CONTENTS

Dedicated to the poets of Marin, past, present and future,
who bring richness to our lives and honor to our home county . . .

And always, to Lee,
who holds my hand in sun and storm.

—⟋⟍—

With thanks to Tom Centolella at whose knee I started writing
poetry and who has been teacher and mentor for many Marin
poets; to Ellery Akers whose encouragement and *WOW*s have been
boundless; to Nancy Binzen and Jerry Fleming for help in seeking
printers; to Nancy Cherry, Greg Darms, Ruth Daigon, Molly Fisk,
Doug Jeffrey, Peter Kunz, Susan Terris, and Jeremy Thornton for
constancy and answers, and to the poets, artists, and photographers
for their willing participation.

And special thanks to Christi Payne Fryday for all the work she did
on book design and disk readiness, for unflappable assistance,
knowledge, and good ideas. All done gratis because of her
enthusiasm for the project.

"Journey to Mount Tamalpais"

SOMETIMES, THEY OPEN A NEW HIGHWAY, AND LET IT ROLL, OPEN WIDE the earth, shake trees from their roots. The Old Woman suffers once more. Birds leave the edges of the forest, abandon the highway. They go up to mountain tops and from the highest peaks they take in the widest landscapes, they even foresee the space age.

The condor is dying. He used to live on the top of Tamalpais. His square wings used to carry him over the area: the hills were moving beneath him with silent pride. He used to cut through the clouds like a fearful knife. At certain seasons he used to carry the moon between his claws. Now we took over his purpose. We are the ones to go to the Mountain. . . .

Like a chorus, the warm breeze had come all the way from Athens and Baghdad, to the Bay, by the Pacific Route, its longest journey. It is the energy of these winds that pushed me when I came to these shores, obsessed, followed by my home-made furies, errynies, and such potent creatures. And I fell in love with the immense blue eyes of the Pacific: I was its red algae, its blood-colored cliffs, its pulsating breath. The ocean led me to the mountain . . .

Year after year, coming down Grand Avenue in San Rafael, coming up from Monterey or Carmel, coming from the north and the Mendocino Coast, Tamalpais appeared as a constant point of reference, the way a desert traveler will see an oasis, not only for water, but as the very idea of home. In such cases geographic spots become spiritual concepts.

The pyramidal shape of the mountain reveals a perfect Intelligence within the universe. Sometimes its power to melt in mist reveals the infinite possibilities for matter to change its appearance.

I watch its colors: they always astonish me. When it is velvet green, friendly, with clear trails, people and animals are invited to climb, to walk, to breathe. When milky white it becomes the Indian goddess it used to be: a huge being with millions of eyes hidden beneath its skin, similar to the image of God which was familiar to me in my childhood days. When it is purple, it radiates.

About three in the afternoon, the mountain starts to swell. The colors and the shadows sharpen. The volumes come into fullness. It all looks so mysterious.

—from the opening section

Every Day

It is not impersonal, the world.
Or strict. If she is awake to every stalk.
If she can watch the hyacinths hammer their green beaks
through the ground.

This was the day of the strong wind, cold, so her pants blew around her
and the herons hunched
and the Bishop Pines shook and shook.

Yesterday the day of sun and crows.

Today the rancher tossed bales off his truck
and the cattle moaned and followed him.

She loves watching the sun as it glazes the trees in the wind.
She is happy, but it true they are happier.

Light showers across them and sprays out of them
every day.

When she has lost everything, that is where she begins.
Think of loss as the earth that covers her
and she the seed.

The day comes towards her and goes away from her again
bringing its cargo of leaves that shine.

How the sea has been a fever in her
and washed her out.

After she has been scoured,
she sits down and praises the minutes.

Every time. Every time she hears a flicker call.
Every time she passes the trees.

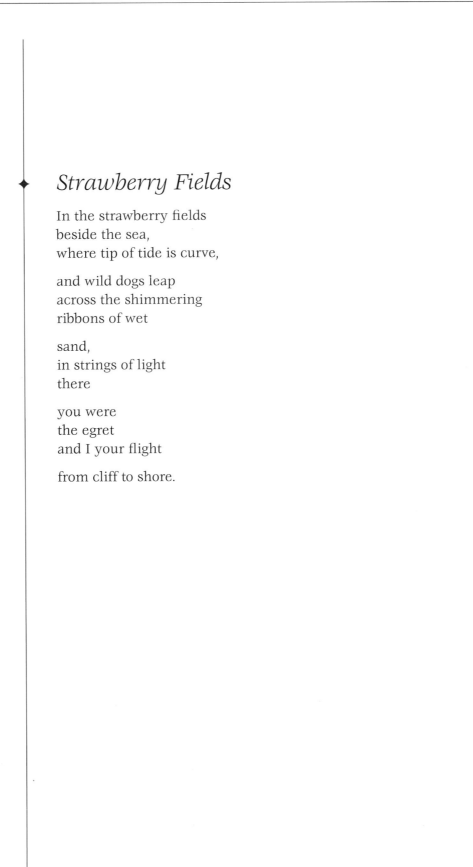

Strawberry Fields

In the strawberry fields
beside the sea,
where tip of tide is curve,

and wild dogs leap
across the shimmering
ribbons of wet

sand,
in strings of light
there

you were
the egret
and I your flight

from cliff to shore.

Looking for Home

They enter my makeshift classroom
with office divider walls and
a lopsided table, not enough
fold-up chairs.
They sit on the floor
and use old National Geographics,
my only teaching supplies,
as miniature table tops.

They are Mexicans, Guatemalans,
anyone I've managed to pull away
from the free clothing room,
saying "Come learn English.
Puede aprender ingles. Today."
They are mainly men my age who
have left their families
to search for jobs and the good life
some *muchacho* passing through
their town had told them about.

They know little more than
"What's up?" and "My name is Daniel."
The first day they laugh
at their own mispronunciations
and my being a woman, muttering
jokes in Spanish, not understanding
the meaning behind my language.
They hear only guttural sounds and
"h"s that, in their country,
would have remained silent.

Each day they come, at first just
a group of noses peeking over the wall
to see if this classroom still exists,
always surprised that I
am still here, have not been deported
like their friends. Each day
there are more questions.
What is the difference
between "know" and "no",
how do you spell "learn"?
Teacher, what does your name mean in Spanish?

They cultivate calm English words
in their mouths, still longing for
the rolling "r"s and the salsa "ch"
of Spanish, still waiting for the day
they'll know how to ask a stranger
directions on the street
rather than wandering the dry,
sun-crackled sidewalks of San Rafael,
hoping to come across a landmark,
something familiar that will
tell them they're home.

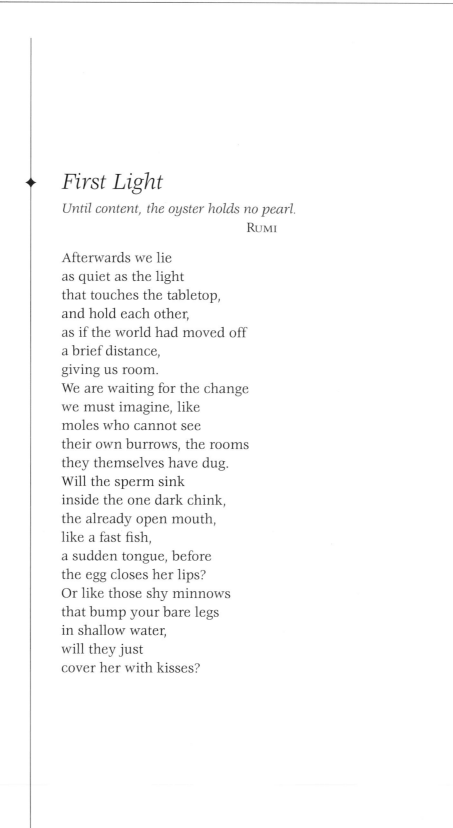

First Light

Until content, the oyster holds no pearl.
                                        RUMI

Afterwards we lie
as quiet as the light
that touches the tabletop,
and hold each other,
as if the world had moved off
a brief distance,
giving us room.
We are waiting for the change
we must imagine, like
moles who cannot see
their own burrows, the rooms
they themselves have dug.
Will the sperm sink
inside the one dark chink,
the already open mouth,
like a fast fish,
a sudden tongue, before
the egg closes her lips?
Or like those shy minnows
that bump your bare legs
in shallow water,
will they just
cover her with kisses?

Musings

I was thinking, this morning,
closely about death
as I dry, here and there,
forever

I wondered if I would wait.
I examined my treasures
I used to fret for fear
they'd not have a new
and proper home, but
this morning I detached
them from me and,
no longer caring, in that way,
I loved them all the more

I put my death back into its place,
not far, but away and then
I heard a phrase,
". . . therefore choose life . . ."
which presupposes one has a choice.
But,
there is a choice,
in a manner of speaking
and, so,
this day
I play
with my choice

Coming Home

Whenever I cross the bridge back,
I look at the mountain, at the craggy cliffs,
remembering the lines
across my father's tan face,
the people he will never meet:
my sleeping, unborn children.
Climbing to the other side,
I walk the leafless paths to your plum tea house.
I walk to your door and pull back the curtains
to the familiar scent of bamboo,
the woven leaves of tatami.
When I have settled onto my cushion,
I watch the steam rise
from the ivory cups you have placed before us.
I watch you, as I once watched my father;
it is then I want to gather the past
into my arms, touch his face,
have him hold me one more time.
But, as I tell you this, you only push the windows open,
look out across the mist-covered mountain
I have climbed, showing me all that I am missing
trying to live the past the way that I do—until I look up
into your dark eyes loving me and bow.

Two Heart Clan

Two Hearts are always first
to send blankets and food to a sing.
Two Hearts know that stolen objects
always go back where they belong.
Two Hearts keep silent when they have
nothing to say, but gossip travels like an arrow.
Two Hearts stay up late at a 49 dance
and wake up bleary-eyed with the sun.
Two Hearts bring venison at mid-winter
to the wind blown lodges of the elders.
Two Hearts die in heat-shimmering prairie grass
and are buried facing east
under piles of red rock.
Two Hearts raise the sun with their prayers
and call deaf-eared rain with gesture
old as rain itself.
Two Hearts never do what they're told
and their children grown up strong steady reeds
impervious to wind.
Two Hearts camp under late summer cottonwoods;
their gray smoke lifts
soft white seed to the sky.
Two Hearts read the winter in a spider web
leaping against its anchoring strands
in the first cool wind of autumn.
A Two Heart life is the journey of a star
from blue evening through black night
to red dawn's horizon.
Two Hearts know we all must die
yet they laugh, they laugh, they laugh.

(*Note:* A 49 dance is held after a regular Powwow and
can often last all night.)

Treading Light #5

◆ *Hodeo*

Harbingers of spring, the green-violet swallows
return each year to the eaves
above the "back-front" door of our house
facing the tripartite brow of White's Hill
(this east facade is face-like, with lobed
appurtenances—"Buddha's
ears," I've called them
half in jest).
Here is where we drew the line, on this southern ridge
of San Geronimo Valley. Here we wrestled through three
mud seasons to build an orgone—
generating structure of fir and redwood, stone, earth, iron
and steel and glass. Into then-wet plaster
on the kitchen wall we impressed
a frieze of native meadow grasses.
The name which came to us
was Dzam Hridayam
Home
meaning, more or less: Be/
come That by the Fiat of the spoken word
which emanates from the heart-cave—

Four times during the first year,
on the solstices and equinoxes
I set up my orange transit over a benchmark on the building's spine
and shot angles to record the sunrise
and sunset alignments,
which I charted as a web of ray
traces on deckrails, walls
and floor—(as if, through surveying
I might demonstrate to my doubting self
how uncanny is this Manifest
of the cosmos, and how quaint and comforting
is the image of an ineffable Geometer
at work)
encompassing the broad enactment of horizon sky
by which we live.

Fecund

Fecund– holding the lips taut
Fecund– under the root
Fecund– a dehydrated heart
dropped with water

Ferns curled in a nub
exploding out
Roots form a teepee
stuck in the earth

I'm upside down
watching this silence
swept by whispers of wind
an occasional caw
hawks circle   drop
               a single
                     spotted
                         clue–
the note of a feather
inside me unfurling
fecund   fecund   fecund

Through the sky light
is the moon in bright sunlight
My mother rests in the ground
My father laughs with his
new woman friend– and
why shouldn't he?
I'm in the skin of the hawk
circling   watching what this
irrepressible God will grant me next
sliding lightly into cool wet
grass sparkling ever
so slightly then
opening–
fecund

Between Women
for *Kathy*

Silver forks glide through lemon cake,
clink against china plates.
Cups filled with fresh brewed coffee rattle
as they settle into saucers.
Reflections of fire play against the window
where rain cascades.

You lean forward on the sofa,
tell me, in a quiet voice,
"I have breast cancer."

Since Sunday, I've known.
Since you phoned to ask, "Can we get together?"
Call it the ancient mystery of women,
silent words that pass between us,
knowing without being told.

Many times, I've seen you fall,
rise again with grace and dignity.
In these dark hours,
you rise, once more, to your finest self.

You smile, hand me a small photo-image
of an unborn child, your grandson,
the breath of air that enters a room
when you're about to suffocate.

The evening passes too quickly,
as it often does when there is
honest, open talk between friends.

The rain stops.
I lean against the door as you leave,
listen to your footsteps
disappear into the night.

I'll think of you tomorrow.
Of the grandson poised to enter your world.
Of you, walking to the Bay at dawn,
opening your coat to the sun,
watching the new day rise around you.

Sidelines

Rattled in the reckoning hour,
dog-day heat still loud as firecrackers,
I am startled by the small figure
of my son jutting from the green field.

The evening mounting around him
like a stadium, he moves in fine circles
chanced on the diamond's edge.
The dust preoccupies him; small wings
distract his sportsman's eye.

In the wise dance we all unlearn,
distinct from the knowing of it,
my son flails the palpable light
and mocks his shadow in tall grasses.

Until, heavy with waiting,
he springs to a run, reaches me and
is past, calling aloud for me
to mark his way in the still, quick dusk:

A kite, ever smaller, pulling away
into the just and cavernous sky.

Whose Laurel Leaves

evergreen   As leaves of grass prove

incensory   I am the word for this vapor

sybilant   Fooled by senseless scribble

or bound by perfect arrow

WOUND

Breaking asparagus stalks

letting their broken stems

fall to the ground

for mice to feed on

there is not too much

AGAINST

At daybreak a hair-raising wind

the trees rise restless

shackled by fear

to greet it

to pause or to pursue

ARCH OF CROWN

Ripe figs under broad leaves

yellow stems snapped

purple skins split open

sweet seeds ravaged by teeth

green sun shining through green air

A Roomy Place

Concrete Land
With hula hoops, Chinese jump ropes, jacks
And crooked-neck pimps on its corners
Squawking furtive propositions of salvation
We children defied their language
And danced
Under the shadow of their wings
As a radio's insistent deliveries of
Bags of hope
Poured music into
Our young and lonely hearts
Echoing refuge
Inside the roomy places
Of our imaginations.

Amorous Trees

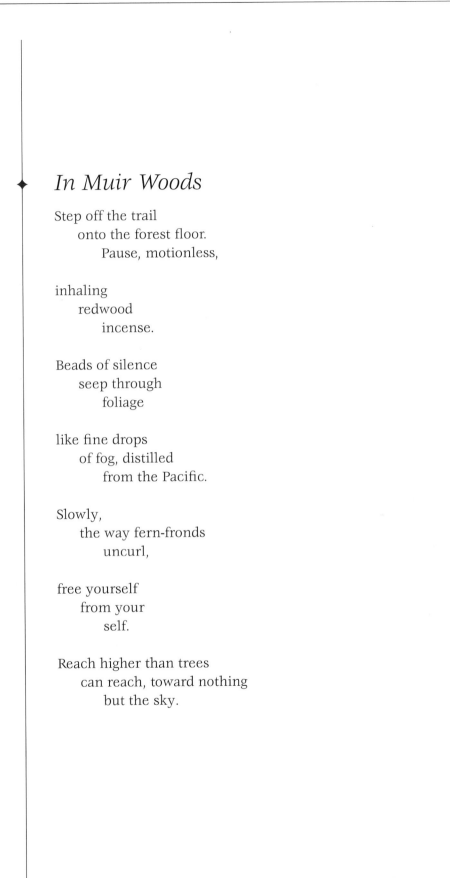

In Muir Woods

Step off the trail
    onto the forest floor.
        Pause, motionless,

inhaling
    redwood
        incense.

Beads of silence
    seep through
        foliage

like fine drops
    of fog, distilled
        from the Pacific.

Slowly,
    the way fern-fronds
        uncurl,

free yourself
    from your
        self.

Reach higher than trees
    can reach, toward nothing
        but the sky.

Our Fabled Lady Eludes the Dragons

"Every breathing sound may seem a prison
and a poison for a moment," Cassandra
ponders as her moving body plays
like a spent moon among trees by a river,
thwarting an evening breeze.

One spirit replies among her selves, "And yet
once you courted the animal desire
and you forgave each merciless glance, and you
applauded those prowling fingers on a thigh
and the scalding whispers at the nape
entreating."

Cassandra says in a murmur,
"I was a daughter yet,
a melancholy wanderer beaming to a foreign star:
unable to possess, too timorous to relent.
In the winter I mourned the flowers of the spring
and sorrowed too sweetly they'd be lost
through the summer, and through autumn."

"O the water emits
an immaculate wizardry."

A Woman's Story

Shadows blow across the dunes
a plainsong of memories
touching, separating
clouds and breasts remember
stars, leaves, children lost
through keyholes, windows
a woman's story
stitched into a mola
held close to her heart
kept under her pillow

CLAUDIA CHAPLINE

Sumi-E, Meditation in Ink

Agate-eyed, he watched us
approach from the east like smoke
from the neighborhood fires—burned
oak and eucalyptus. We drifted
with the same wind as we walked to Shell Beach.
And the low-beamed sky
spread gray with the rain that curls
back on itself to become hail.
But before the hail, we arrive
 at the deer, ears, a twitch of leaf or stroke
of wind in the grass he has made
into a nest with nettle and blood.
From the west, before the hail
we watch the deer, his eyelids low
as curtains pulled in an afternoon
sick room, his hide stiff
as the Japanese brush you use
to create *kanji* —ink that speaks
in all directions. In the turn
that bends north toward homes,
the young buck curls back
upon himself, raises his head
a few degrees south as we approach.
He must smell our human scent
of salt sweat and soap.
We come upon him at the center
of our conversation, his brow
the color of sand wet at low tide, antlers
still covered in that spring moss, a rack
that would branch and point in all four
directions if he lived. But he would not
live. Mangled by some forgotten fender,
hind leg snapped and shattered. The bone
bare from joint to thigh, ribbons
of tendon exposed to February
as blood leaks down the damp leather
of his nose. Even as we watch, his chest

heaves beneath ribs that hold like a fist;
then the trot of breath, quick-pant,
mouth open only enough to release a hiss
of warm air. His ears tilt west
as they might have had he stood
in our garden, startled by any human
presence. A deer ready to dart
in the opposite direction.
Could we lift him out of the hollow
he has made; could we turn away?
At the kitchen table, you spread out paper,
parchment of pressed mulberry
and take down the brush, open ink
and begin with *mizu,* water,
the stroke that begins every word—
first down then north, up and west, *water*
with the tick at the top for *eternal.*
Beyond our window, the buckeye points
its first leaves south in the rain of fire,
north in the rain of earth.

GREG DARMS

The Chinook Arrives on Fourth Street
(Chinook: the warm wind which brings the first thaw of Spring)

The bees came slipping into a moment
chiseled from a long golden afternoon
gray at the edges with a promise of fog.

Even the pigeons stopped their incessant
circles, stopped tossing dead bits of leaf
as if they expected loaves to float down.

The pigeons stood still on their naked pink feet
and the toddlers in bright overalls ceased
their centrifugal bouncing. In the shops,

behind the plate glass, faces settled in rows
mouths forming silent-film **O**'s.
Chewing stopped on the sidewalk café.

Heads tilted to watch, traffic came to a halt
in the pause between red and green
and the rattle of engines dulled like a shell

held to the ear, the hum of the bees swirled
down to the street like an angry black fog.
Ragged streamers twirled tighter, condensed

to a liquid black mass dripping in clots
from a manicured tree in a tub. Like a color
at the edge of perception their buzz

filled the street, nearly subsonic.
An uneasy mosaic of bees re-created the tree
while above the sign claimed *Chinook!*

I must stop planning my life.

We Don't Have to Share a Fate

We don't have to share a fate,
we don't have to draw shameful conclusions.

After the shutter releases,
I want you in the plural,

in the snake carriage,
in the glacier room,

in the closet full
of guitars and stomped hay,

in the exhalation of others,
all swaying with love, but changing midway

through the words
I address to you, my hand

pressed to yours visibly
much paler

than before, an orchid
offered beneath a warring sky,

an orchid that yawns
and cracks open and falls apart

unexpected in a bed of soft clothes,
where your shoulders become two steps,

dawns fruits rivers and knives,
full glottal, wide lens,

and your hands become two countries,
and my legs murmured like grass,

a dumb love,
a tether to all dreams of enduring,

long convoy between two powers
killing the mockery of words

while daylight floats,
orchids, white dogs stretched out between the slow-burning lanterns.

Priority Mail for My Sons

I mailed you an extra year
from another country
where wooden sidewalks
end in cinder paths

where privies lean
a little more each year
and morning light falls
weightless on rain barrels.

Enclosed you'll find a Chevy
with running boards
a Burma Shave sign
that points the way you'll

travel years from now.
I've wrapped with care
the smell of citronella
camphor and cod liver oil

the gramophone scratching out
Hi-Di-Hi's and Bye-Bye-Blues
A blade of grass to whistle through
a fortress at the beach

a woolen bathing suit that
shrinks an inch each season.
It's just arrived and waiting
at the back door of your life.

The Tug

Fox three feet above ground caught
in willow scrub, his small rag of body
flag at half.
Buds on bent stems,
soft hairs.
When the creek receded, grasses
pointed out the way the current
has insisted.
Nettles sprang from flood silt green as ever.
Leaves comfortably unfolded.
The fox was completely lost in the air.
A boat had washed over the levee.
No one could get it back.

SPAIN: Flamenco

MARIO: Guitarist

Pineapple on a window sill
In the early a. m. of Spain.
(Sun by Matisse).

I hear the shimmer of trills,
High grass, and river flowing with shawl fringe.

Water rippling through guitar strings,
Giving promises that God is a Lady
With a rose in her hair and perfume
       At her breasts.

CHENIN: Singer

The coarse edge to his big voice.
The whole land, like moldy earth,
Held in his closed hands.

(I taste Spain under my tongue)

His sound shapes itself around the words
And they fall away from inside, leaving
Empty, crying, spaces.

LOURDES: Dancer

Beyond her heels, the click of details:
Head, hands, eye, skirt, fan, shawl, shoulders,
       hips,
Ripple from her center, touch on each other,
       Never overlap.

Or she pauses, holding stillness in her body.
Then bends low,
In a long curve, shawl outstretched behind her,
A great bird's wing slowly turns.

Whole Moon Bluely

The Pacific comes in at an angle
San Francisco smoked orange & hovers
moon glown over foam
seizes a sidewise heave
lunar gnashing water, a sea luscious thrust
waves in backlash rebuttals
the lovely drivel of Bolinas elders
slivers of silver
each curling wave ignites its precious squint
smacks the shale base way
a reef crammed with current submersions
rousts rooster tails of aerial spume
sprung off and against flushed cliffs
March is frosty if
clutch attempts the benighted naught
high tide stars aswoop in articles
loose circles at self
a reference to the sea my midnight swallows.

Coast Hills, Mt. Tam Toward San Francisco

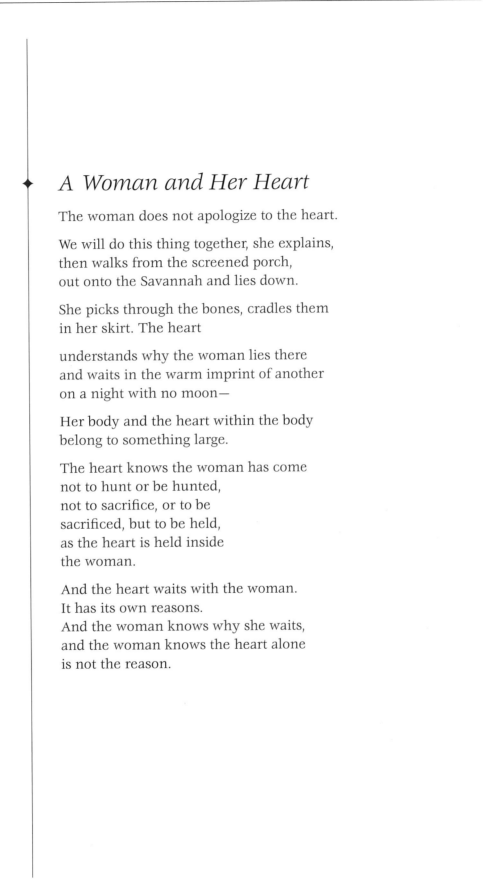

A Woman and Her Heart

The woman does not apologize to the heart.

We will do this thing together, she explains,
then walks from the screened porch,
out onto the Savannah and lies down.

She picks through the bones, cradles them
in her skirt. The heart

understands why the woman lies there
and waits in the warm imprint of another
on a night with no moon—

Her body and the heart within the body
belong to something large.

The heart knows the woman has come
not to hunt or be hunted,
not to sacrifice, or to be
sacrificed, but to be held,
as the heart is held inside
the woman.

And the heart waits with the woman.
It has its own reasons.
And the woman knows why she waits,
and the woman knows the heart alone
is not the reason.

After a Certain Age a Woman Becomes Invisible

Her foundation will begin to shift
roof tiles curl
rain seep in.
At first she won't observe herself:
the crisp curve of edges eroding
white sheets no longer hanging on her line
like an invitation.

All too soon she will notice
the restless eyes
that pass through her without stopping.
She will mourn her loss,
putty and caulk
paint and plaster
but the decay
will go faster than the repair.
One day while working
she may lean back to admire the job,
and if lucky,
see as if for the first time
her elegant structure.

She will be able then to let go
the old ladders
they will no longer matter.
She will peel back her roof
and become a garden,
open up
and hold the rain.

Ruins

You are beautiful in your bones,
an arrangement of angles without shadow,
existing in two dimensions,
a fallen architecture no longer bearing weight,
enduring ruin.

In the early morning light,
I draw the sheet to cover you.
You turn your face to the window
where the pale sun filters
across the sill. You turn your face
as if to receive a blessing,
having fallen.
Pain has eroded your body
as wind erodes stone,
and water, earth.

You are beautiful in your bones,
as the ruins of an ancient city
are beautiful, buried
under sudden ash
with all its people fallen.
When the alarm sounded, fallen
in gestures of life,
drawing water, buying pomegranates,
shielding a child,
running . . .

Anthem

I have heard this music before,
saith the body.

—Mary Oliver

Always the heart repeats its true name.
The twin bellows of lung fill and soften, and soften
further, and fill, a song heard in the pines,
in the eaves of houses emptied in summer—
a gurgle of laughter, water. I am alone,
like the fox, alert on an unused road, still.
Listening. Wild radish and lupine, larkspur,
and grasses: bright flags of the generous world.
And since *yes* requires its answering *no*:
the snapped neck of a deer splayed half-across the path
and a pair of raucous crows. Farther along, something,
a vole or hapless mouse, gathered and dispersed
in the delicate cough ball of an owl.
This is when it gets difficult: learning how to live.
A sliver of burnished ocean sings beyond the hills
and the sturdy heart blesses its own reflection.

The Beekeeper's Beard

The beekeeper's beard, having only every hue of grey bound intricately into its great length, depends on bees & sun to make it blonde again. These Saturday mornings in Luxembourg Gardens, the faithful gather around him in their wide hats & veils, as tomorrow they will gather in St. Sulpice, St. Severin, St. Julian le Pauvre, if only to hear the organ & breathe the air given up by the stone floor. His voice, too, is taken from such air and warmed, and on these mornings of instruction sent out in easy spirals to his followers, a music his hands move to as they demonstrate the extraction of honey, the removal of trays, the introduction of the queen to her hive.

One day, perhaps not even in this decade, his beard will have grown fully to his toes; and a certain afternoon in Yvelines, full with sun & the yellowness of bees & the iridescent wings beating, he will be done.

His wife will look out from the shade of the kitchen & whisper: *So, Michel: the long dream of your daughter's hair is attained. She sang, too, like those wings, and claimed one season whose flowers were the sweetest anyone in the Societé Centrale Apiculture can remember.*

Bull Kelp

1.

Beyond South Beach, the bull kelp snap from their holdfasts
and are carried away loose as fingers through the surf.
Massive waves pound the steep slant of shore,
their hum and growl shaking the sand into dense flanks.

High tides and on-shore winds
fill the beach with the floats and rubbery stipes
of bull whips
that turn to leather in the straight-on sun.

Tugging at bleached white, amber, or raw sienna whips,
I covered that beach, looking for color and length,
while the dogs sectioned the sand with tracks,
racing stripes of slather along their dark bodies.

In the small convertible
I piled great snarls of kelp
back seat, front, the trunk,
so that for the ride home the dogs
had to nest in it like plump geese.

2.

I put it in the basement
with other basket material.
Then came the year we lost so much,
and had to sell the house. Under deadline,

I worked my way from the once-children's rooms at the top
to the "someday" room in the basement.
A slag heap formed on the deck.

Twice a week the handyman came with his pick up
and made a run to the dump:
shelves of beachcombing, art projects,
rusted gears and sprockets, collage scraps
a shopping bag of broken car glass.

There'd be no "someday" room wherever we were going
and so I came to the tangled kelp,
hauled its cumbersome Gordian clump out to the deck.

3.
Its colors, its long tapered stalks, the goofy bald globes,
stiff now but still beautiful, brought
that wild, wet, briny day on South Beach in like storm combers.
The sound returned, the joyful dogs, the straight
line of beach that crammed its point into the Pacific.

I dragged the whole knot off the pile, and worked
my way through, disengaging each whip,
laying them out like exclamation points.

I thought of the kelp gripping the sub-tidal bottom,
their floats sometimes a fishing raft for heron.
How great storms had caused them to lose their hold
and follow the whim of tides.

With razor-sharp scissors I cut and saved
every possible piece, and for the next five hours
sat on the boards of the deck, dogs by my side,
and made baskets, one after the other,
working that salty weft around and around.

The Bee Trophy

The dust of Marin fireroads in late summer,
early fall—before the rains—is so fine
you can read the smallest imprint
from the bottoms of shoes that have recently
passed. It's more than possible
to meet yourself coming from where
you're going back to, once you recognize
your own footprints in the dust.

If I were to introduce my self to my former self,
I would—and often do—stop to converse.
Here is where the footprints paused
and turned to the side of the road,
noticing bumble bee asleep in the thistle.
And here is where I pause
to see if the bee still sleeps. Here
we both laugh, remembering the first
discovery of sleeping bee,
and how we thought it dead,
and wouldn't it be nice
to carry home a bee trophy,
because we often carry home
treasures from the trail, and how
we bent and sawed at thistle stem,
and how the bee waved in the air
from our efforts, and how something,
possibly the slightest, slowest
movement from the insect
led us to think that maybe
this was not dead bee at all.
How we marked the place in the trail,
to look another day,
to find either dead bee or nothing,
and left it—bent stem on which it clung—
to wake or to die peacefully.
How since then we have noticed bees,
sleeping bees,
but only in the early morning,
tucked into thistles, stiff from the cold,
waiting for the sun to revive them.

The Roly Poly Bug

One by one they appear through the crack
of my front door.
Native roly polies—pill or sow bug
with perfectly curled armor
as they roll themselves into a knot.
Harmless little legs—baby moustaches
attached to their bodies
and their gray shells with aligned segments
like one hundred miniature armies inside them
that never go to war but keep marching.
Here they come, one, two, three
little roly polies rolling along,
curling up not to sleep but to protect
their bodies from invasion of the brush of my broom.
The broom misses.

I declare them the totem animal of Pixie Trail.
I put on my roly poly mask in celebration
of this aikido warrior of the crustacean world.

Marks Which Darken or Let in Light
For Marie Carbone

The ruled line is lifeless, the compass, a deadly cultivation. A circle or her segment holds no gift unless the marker feelingly molds the form. She begins with a demurrer: the body is meddlesome as drapes, any elegance diminished, that is, against the urge to become adoring. In a motion of supplication and hope, the assent may even be the interest, the profile of a blossom in its chronology, the tenacious quality of the sky. She draws the music up to her, it composes another small room, now emptying, now entering, the texture of that vessel cracked and therefore open. Olympia, Eve, labeled Leda or Ida, Venus moving forward as a flurry of tulips, breath curving, kissing, speaking signs and blankness to be filled as wished with the invisible. When it is once done, the spinning of the circle which does not weave has only a breathless, dizzying purpose. Calm Goddess, effervescent space forms from the impurities of the vessel. A theorem: schoolgirl stencils, some force and daring, some free drawing. The flowers are confabulating when one is nineteen or twenty or twenty-two, we scatter ourselves ceaselessly in disorderly deeds. (Whoever spends years sewing white anemones cannot be distracted.) Parens or plenum of pillow breast petal leaf broke bowl, gold joints of the stellar medallion, a plethora of exclamations like the sun, like sperm cruising the central egg. An egg in the old sense is not possible. The most radiant is gilded, the mostly beautiful, cold stone. Her throne's not the bed nor the pedestal. Her metic tracery in the labyrinth, testy yet ardent for the unconditioned, the evident, for placid resisting urgency, a repose and a rushing. There is sustenance, Breathing Lotus, there is rest. The present has its back to us, faced only in remove. Realm of consolation, of shame, of pain and possible healing, far along in this scattering. A space, or all space, every part of which holds the full, speckled distance of the revenant, of stars hinged in their constellations—I might agree to call this my freedom.

my desire   *my universe*   *my memory*   *my cure*

Fishing in the Keep of Silence

There is a hush now while the hills rise up
and God is going to sleep. He trusts the ship
of Heaven to take over and proceed beautifully
as he lies dreaming in the lap of the world.
He knows the owls will guard the sweetness
of the soul in their massive keep of silence,
looking out with eyes open or closed over
the length of Tomales Bay that the herons
conform to, whitely broad in flight, white
and slim in standing. God, who thinks about
poetry all the time, breathes happily as He
repeats to Himself: There are fish in the net,
lots of fish this time in the net of the heart.

JOYCE LIVINGSTON

A Story About the Body

The young composer, working that summer at an artist's colony, had watched her for a week. She was Japanese, a painter, almost sixty, and he thought he was in love with her. He loved her work, and her work was like the way she moved her body, used her hands, looked at him directly when she made amused and considered answers to his questions. One night, walking back from a concert, they came to her door and she turned to him and said, "I think you would like to have me. I would like that too, but I must tell you that I have had a double mastectomy," and when he didn't understand, "I've lost both my breasts." The radiance that he had carried around in his belly and chest cavity—like music—withered very quickly, and he made himself look at her when he said, "I'm sorry. I don't think I could." He walked back to his own cabin through the pines, and in the morning he found a small blue bowl on the porch outside his door. It looked to be full of rose petals, but he found when he picked it up that the rose petals were on top; the rest of the bowl—she must have swept them from the corners of her studio—was full of dead bees.

P.M. – 1919 / A.M. – 1993

P.M. – 1919

He slips out of the second-story bedroom window,
scrambles down the side of the house
and across the dark yard
to the hidden downhill corner of the lot
to scoop up the new-found puppy
and carry it back to the house.
His older brother lowers a basket on a rope
and once again they sneak the puppy up to their room.
Their mother would kill them
if she knew they had a dog.
He snuggles deep into the scratchy wool blankets,
the little hound in his arms
pressed up tight to his ribcage,
can feel its heart beating against his,
drifts off to the rise and fall
of its soft breathing.

A.M. – 1993

He's awakened by the pain,
calls out from the rented hospital bed
in the middle of the living room.
Then waits for the drug to swallow him up.
And what was he dreaming about?
His sister . . .
hasn't thought about her in years,
easier not to,
never liked to think about the madness.
But the old Sausalito house . . .
His daughter has been asking
to hear the stories again –

(continued)

of Sleepy Alfonso and the horse-drawn milkwagon,
and how Mason's Garage
ran a distillery during Prohibition,
and the one about Jim Doyle's brother
driving a loaded truck onto the ferry,
but something went wrong with the ramp
and both the truck and the brother
wound up in San Francisco Bay. . . .
Damn! When would the pain let up?
He remembers a puppy he and his brother
smuggled up to their room each night . . .
He'd have to check with his daughter,
see if he already
told her that one.

Mighty Forms

◆

The earth had wanted us all to itself.
The mountains wanted us back for themselves.
The numbered valleys of serpentine wanted us;
that's why it happened as it did, the split
as if one slow gear turned beneath us . . .
Then the Tuesday shoppers paused in the street
and the tube that held the trout-colored train
and the cords of action from triangular buildings
and the terraced gardens that held camellias
shook and shook, each flower a single thought.

Mothers and children took cover under tables.
I called out to her who was my life.
From under the table—I hid under the table
that held the begonia with the fiery stem,
the stem that had been trying to root, that paused
in its effort—I called to the child who was my life.
And understood, in the endless instant
before she answered, how Pharaoh's army, seeing
the ground break open, seeing the first fringed
horses fall into the gap, made their vows,
that each heart changes, faced with a single awe
and in that moment a promise is written out.

However we remember California later
the earth we loved will know the truth:
that it wanted us back for itself
with our mighty forms and our specific longings,
wanted them to be air and fire but they wouldn't;
the kestrel circled over a pine, which lasted,
the towhee who loved freedom, gathering seed
during the shaking lasted, the painting released
by the wall, the mark and hook we placed
on the wall, and the nail, and the memory
of driving the nail in, these also lasted—

The Love of Aged Horses

Because I know tomorrow
his faithful gelding heart will be broken
when the spotted mare is trailered and driven away,
I come today to take him for a gallop on Diaz ridge.

Returning, he will whinny for his love.
Ancient, spavined,
her white parts red with hill-dust,
her red parts whitened with the same, she never answers.

But today, when I turn him loose at the bent gate
with the taste of chewed oat on his tongue
and the saddle-sweat rinsed off with water,
I know he will canter, however tired,
whinnying wildly up the ridge's near side,
and I know he will find her.

He will be filled with the sureness of horses
whose bellies are grain-filled,
whose long-ribbed loneliness
can be scratched into no-longer-lonely.

His long teeth on her withers,
her rough-coated spots will grow damp and wild.
Her long teeth on his withers,
his oiled-teakwood smoothness will grow damp and wild.
Their shadows' chiasmus will fleck and fill with flies,
the eight marks of their fortune stamp and then cancel the earth.
From ear-flick to tail-switch, they stand in one body.
No luck is as boundless as theirs.

At Stinson

At the end of a road,
a few gray boards lean
towards the loft of stars.

After the sun has set
and the last nasturtiums close
like breaking waves, we do

what's not allowed—tent
together sticks, crumple
the news, and let

the wind swirl embers
into the sky: a new constellation
that keeps changing

and doesn't have a name.
Later, we rub our bodies together
like sticks. From our bed, I see stars

go out like scattered coals.
The hills are strewn
with cars, people sprawled

on the warm hoods, staring up
at the sky where a few cinders
shower back to earth.

Nine Generations Lost

I

They say you
couldn't hear me because I'm a woman and hide in
the woods to learn Hebrew
while my Father and six brothers died blazing
leaving me to escape. . . .
My fiancé killed at the Russian border/
forward to the next life
in America's haunted streets

II

I was born the year Israel was born
but nobody told me who I was or
why you were gone

children, I don't want to die
return and swing your little feet along the path,
play with your friends and
live the love they took from you

SIX MILLION TIMES
I died before I was born

III

So my love   you died   before I woke
I am a Jew and I am glad)
the sad rustling of your instinctive gathering
of facts, forcing me to cry
in the night because they were all greedy and spiteful
twisting my face and turning my smile—

STOP, hold your fear, I saw my Mother return to life
and almost was held back against glasslike pain

turning to flowers again.

Engkanto

It is spring today and I think of you kneeling
beside me, this man who was my father's father,
who appeared one day and stayed until
I learned your habits, how you dressed

like an old relative all day in flannel pajamas,
with your slippers shuffling down the back stairs
to the garden where you'd disappear, crouched
like a troll, casting spells among the leaves

and branches, reciting an old language
I'd later forget. *Araw araw, unti unti*, you'd
say before you began the long afternoons,
bunching leaves, tamping the soil, brushing away

the soggy crumbs of moss as I mimicked you and
flicked away the hollow shells of dead beetles.
Now years later when I'm nearly asleep, listening
to the slow movements of animals, to the rustle

of leaves where their paws might fall, you return,
ancient, waving your leathery hands. I can hear
you so clearly, whispering into my ear, a voice
full of secrets I'll keep like slivers of moonlight.

Note: *araw-araw, unti-unti*—Tagalog for "day by day, little by little"

Fog, Coast Hills, Mt. Tam

Summer Fog in Bolinas

In a white stillness the mesa floats
and out of the fog above a hidden sea
I hear the foghorn's mournful notes
and see a dew-spangled
blue lupine bush in flower
and eucalyptus trained by wind,
a leaning tower.

Fog thickens
phantom dogs run and vanish
and barbed wire strung with dew-beads
marks the pasture
where ghostly cows stand still
knee deep in mist
and stare and silently chew.

Fog thins, wears through
to blue above my head
and through the glimmer and swirl
I don't see the road at all,
the bare brown ruts,
for I'm walking now inside a pearl.

Emigré

Forty years lived in the same place,
you come to know the names for things—
clapboard, sugar maple, Nor'easter
yours as much as *sky* or *mother.*

When I was six, it was nothing
to read music, to speak French,
to memorize the names of clouds.
Now I am slower. Now I live in a new place,
where the sun sets over water,
and I can almost remember what it was like
before I knew the name for water.
Acacia, ice plant, Dungeness crab—
people teach me the words,
but in my mouth they feel like
sudden extra teeth.

Above the trees two dark birds
spiral up to catch the last rapture of the sun.
Hawks, maybe.
Could it be a blessing
not to know their name?
Even to know they are birds
may give too much away—
better to see them as they are,
before thought or language,
before reducing their grace
to what I think I know.

For Ugly Babies

"What an ugly baby,"
      her father cooed.
"Yes, the very ugliest,"
      her mother replied.
"And look into those eyes,
      obviously she is very stupid too."
"Yes, very stupid."
      They said this so that the goblins
      would not be jealous and steal their baby.

      When she had a baby of her own,
      she could not be wise.
"You are the most beautiful baby,"
      she whispered when no one could hear.
"The most beautiful baby
      with the most beautiful eyes and
you will always be happy."
      She was silent, helpless, when the baby
      was taken from her and sent overseas.

      Her daughter grew up an American,
      a writer with poems for children.
      She can be mother and father
      and they will always be hers.
"You're very ugly,"
      she says to one. To another,
"Very beautiful."

Two Views

Their heads almost indistinguishable
from the dots of foam,
sailors in Hokusai's color print
stare up at the torrent,
the knowledge of what shall befall them
arcing over them, caught
for this instant in the hollow of the wave,
as we, mid-way through this course of chemo,
hanging onto the present,
see through the window in Sunday rain
a tulip magnolia like a Japanese print,
petals scattered on the deck below.

What the men on the boat might see
if they turn their gaze to land,
Mt. Fuji in the distance.
Here, Mt. Tam beyond the magnolia
and possibility—we may ride out
the wave, be spared again.

To Ken Kesey's Leading Lady

no matter how many times I stab the control buttons
pause/still what's coming, shout goddamn you, don't threaten him
crush him into cowardice with his heavy mother
he wasn't choking on his words anymore, he'd picked his eyes
off the floor, shined them into your unflinching face, how could you
see your way to bully this blue-eyed man, straighten his unruly curls?
his gaze, knowing, should have softened your chiseled face,
toppled the cap from your rigid hair-do,
heat steaming that crazy blond helmet, unfurling like peace after war,
falling to dye and loosen the virginal cocoon of your uniform
couldn't you have smiled, grasped his hand, scampered into the office
and snagged a bottle from Scatman, stacked a few platters on that
tired turntable, your feet, shoulders, hips revolving like a hit single
couldn't you feel something growing,
not inflating yourself to fit the cloak of authority,
but a heat, a swell,
your buttons, straps, white shoes too much a barrier from life,
shedding, springtime wings
raising young Bibbitt up, strong and full of purpose
but still in charge of him,
"Your mother is a good friend of mine"
setting a different truth on your face
his waist strings yanked for the second time
to hell with having him locked in a sterile examination room
to fret and slash himself with guilt
couldn't you offer a human touch this time,
even Chief wavered, let his guard down, accepted and gave
the greatest kindness he could
I pause and hope, make some tea, smoke
always when I return I press the same button I always press
the one that sets you back on course
to blue-eyed Billy dead in a frozen red puddle

Gliders, Mt. Tamalpais

Power Outage

Once you've seen mud
move, whole hillsides
shimmy, slip seaward,
once you've heard
earth give, settle,
make its own small
corrections, you know
how tenuous any toe-
hold here can be.

Once you've seen
love fall away,
vanish in a bandaged
word, a clattering
silence, you lose all
disposition toward
long views, hold
tight to the near
at hand. All day

long, while rain
lapped posts below
our floor boards,
toppled power poles
above, I simmered
Taki's chicken soup
over a low gas
flame. Tonight,

together, we sit
down by candlelight
to sip the hot of it
from steaming bowls,
along with crusty
bread, arugula, and
good Greek wine.

Clerestory Windows

It's long after Christmas
but some lights are still up
stragglers who won't take them down
or can't.
Victoria sat at the dining room table
only yesterday
and packed the tree stand
and the papier mâché reindeer,
a thousand ornaments and garlands,
she let it all go, reluctantly,
back into its boxes,
Christmas music on the CD player,
hot cider in a mug on the table.
She stretched the season out one last
January morning.

I'm at what used to be
the Mystic Coffee House without you.
Across the street, in the winter dusk,
the old Post Office building
blazes with shop lights.
Its row of clerestory windows
shines out onto the branches of bare trees,
night falling so matter-of-factly
maybe only I notice.

I wish I could reach back
forty miles over the spare hills
and pull you here.
So we could sit together
as the town put on this sable coat.
I wish you could know for certain
how the love I have for you
shines out onto the path between us,
how I look across each
trough of wave
and see your starboard running lights
always on the dark sea.

Once there were true love and friendship,
separate as oil and water.
Now there is how we are together.
And I have no name to give it
or reason for its being
—only that one night like this
we asked ourselves
into each other's lives
and there, for all the good it does us,
we stay.

JOYCE LIVINGSTON

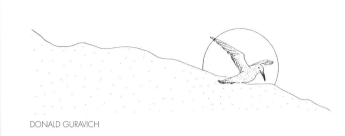

DONALD GURAVICH

In Memorium

First, there were the FIRST PEOPLE
And then the first people made the ANIMALS
And then the ANIMALS made Our People

And this is Memorial Day   weekend with unusual
        rainy overcast skies,   tide the lowest
In twenty years causing the Agate Beach parking lot
        to overflow with cars and their human content
        visiting this Ocean withdrawal phenomena
much advertised by the media. Place to go to, Kids.
        All camouflage revealed in air. You know what I mean—
It's the littoral zone. Where human feet can squish
        the living daylights out of cowering anemones
And the local boys can *walk* to the furthest reef pool
        pick up their abalone and go home.
            So far out, this a view to be seen
Inside the flight of 70 black brants that didn't
want to move,   they didn't *want* to move.

Sonnet

A hummingbird pecks out my eyes, drinks
the blue light from them like water. Another
puts her long beak into my honeysuckle ear
and sucks mind out like black ink.
A third, ruby-throated, with her needle
sews my mouth shut tight.
Blind now, instantly I see.
Deaf, the music of silence
fills me like a fuchsia.
Speechless, I speak true words.
I know no way to write them here,
words made of hummingbirds' wings:
how to hold still while flying,
how to think while not thinking.

What Bird Would Light

—extended, a pier reaching out to the bay, my
hand passes through without
resistance. Like science, everything
has an explanation. And another. This
is how I greet you: each word its own
antecedent. Time knows only
how to repeat itself: here it is
July again, unstoppable as recognition.
What bird would light in a moving tree—
watch for the bird or wait for the tree?
I make a house out of my hands and take
cover there.

                At the lake, the water thickens
to tempt you. I respond
in increments, an asker's portion.
What does she see: the one with eyes
all over her body? Sieving light through each
aperture, perception comes only through the skin.
The gulls, unnamed and abstract, take
flight with them when they go. Home inseparable
from motion. Is this what existence is? Calling out—
and then calling again? No one is more
human than any other. You
have reminded me of you.

Note: *What bird would light in a moving tree* is a quote from Lorine Niedecker.

Thickets

I am studying the quirkiness of thickets,
the eccentricity of massed twigs,
the winter trees whose leaves
lie listless on the ground

like dead fish in a drained pond.
Some thickets are like lace
made by a lunatic,
others so ordered

only a perfectionist god
could have designed them.
Some are at cross purposes,
branches shooting hither and yon.

Oh! And some, the willows,
are the rosy hue of sunsets
scribbled on the sky.
Now, I am painting the thickets,

struggling with their eccentricity,
challenged by their discordant lines
jumbled like notes on a crazy scale.
But only nature, that ultimate artist,

with her fine and wanton brush
can paint the saffron cross-hatching
along our streams and marshes –
those willow thickets, bare.

JOYCE LIVINGSTON

Drying Wings

Wings of Victory

Mary tells of the road near Point Reyes
where, in the late Forties, a farmer
strung on wire fencing hawks and owls
he shot, making this a better place,
a nation free of winged predators.
She remembers that farmer on his tractor
in failing light, outline on the horizon,
mowing dry grass, and asks aloud, I wonder,
did he go to fight in the last great war
and return to clear the air of birds that hunt?

Driving through the treeless pastureland,
past the farm's gate, tied there
on either side, a display of drab kites,
outstretched wings that a quick gust lifts
and holds, barbed wire swaying with its wash
of pinned feathers and wing bone—
How many did you count, and what birds
among them? I see sparrow hawk, osprey
(plentiful then), a snowy owl, any number
of migratory birds, for doesn't this road
bisect the coastal flyway? This fence, Mister,
your billboard. You do yourself proud.

Was such a slaughter of human-interest news?
Perhaps a photo of the boastful farmer
made the *Light,* propped by his gate,
cradling his twelve-gauge, or did he
bring them down with a small-bore stick
of a rifle? Was he that good a marksman,
a sniper on some South Pacific island?
For him, what kills you kill, no holds barred.
Maybe he learned this in that other theater
overseas. Now I ask you, Mary, too late
to make a difference, was there no hue,
no cry, no scream as each raptor fell
in that mown field, in that dim light?

Hatted

First he said he didn't want to be married to me any more,
then he bought me a hat—black felt, brim wide, turned out
like wings, and a crown,
slightly creased, snugged my head.
We admired me in mirrors, painted glass,
others' faces, even eyes hiding
behind brims.

It was at a street fair, warm, end of summer,
lights everywhere—like
India heavy with strings of bulbs—turned night
to a slightly sinister day; I strutted, the way
you do when you know people admire you—one man
applauded, another shouted, "Eva laGalliane."

We held hands, ate mocha chip ice cream,
later beer and hot dogs, continued to hold hands.
On that windless night, the hat stuck like a great disguise.

That night we made love with all the lights on,
as if we were still at the street fair or in India,
as if everything wouldn't be different tomorrow.
The last thing I removed was the hat.

Uncharted Flight

Three hawks circle above us:

    their shadows
break up over
        wooden chairs
          fan over stones
      disappear between cracks in the sidewalk
          tickle grass blades lightly

and glide over the face of the old poet
        who is lifted
out of arthritic joints
    out of asthmatic lungs

for one moment the fresh breeze
      lifts her to a height beyond pain
beyond the fact of her aging
    into the ease and relief of the updraft.

She becomes the fourth hawk,
    finding words in their flight
      to slip inside her wing portfolio.

Through layers of clouds
    she tosses me a few lines
      She says each poem
        is like a shutter clicking
photos of those shadows.

I love to watch her rise with the hawks,
    in each telling
      her poems lift her again and again

      to the freedom of their circling.

Bolinas Lagoon April 1996

I owe you a debt of thanks.
You were the first one who accepted me.
Didn't mold me, make me into an ideal.
You let me be and so I found myself.
By happenchance I'm at Bolinas Lagoon
where we scattered your ashes.
Odd I should be here twenty years to the day
you disappeared over the horizon
like the grey whales offshore.
It wasn't planned. Spring break, a need to get
away. Stinson was perfect. I'd forgotten
the connection until I followed the beach
to the lagoon. A minus tide. Sandbars.
Spines, shallows, burnished rocks, luminescent shells,
sandpipers. A lady bug sunned herself
on a saffron stone.   I thought of you.

Pronouncement

Even when the rain
   slaps the puddles like a smacking
      open palm, and the wind-

cracked air splinters
   limbs, sets them wheeling,
      and the bloated creek

groans beneath its
   own muddy weight,
      still

the narcissus rises up,
   slender green
      magician, sleek

as a knife edge, sturdy
   as hope,
      it rises, unnoticed,

until yellow pools
   of sunlight
      announce: It's come.

It's come, like the final shudder
   after birth's capricious
      opening; the stunned glad song

when grasping
   turns to grace. Say it:
      It's come.
      It's come.

Love Pirates

I follow with my mouth
the small wing of muscle
just under your shoulder,
lean forward over your back
breathing into your hair
and thinking of nothing.
I want to lie down with you
in the bottom of a big canoe
and drift away from all of it,
our two cars rusting quietly
in the parking lot, our families
whining like tame geese
at feeding time,
and all the bosses of the earth
cursing the freeway traffic
in the morning haze.

They will telephone each other
anxiously from their corduroy sofas
and their glass desks,
with no idea where we could be,
unable to imagine the dark throat
of the saxophone playing upriver,
or the fire we gather between us
on this fantail of dusty light,
having stolen a truckload of roses
and thrown them into the sea.

Astrolabe

The moon wanes
with all of our vanished powers,
comes to one side of the day
to complete its series.

Slight as a memory that once said
"locket" or "silver spoon",
the last of the quarters
vanishes in thin air.

Goodbye to the man-made satellite—
that brave trash. At odds with time
an accident falls inward,
into ourselves—ourselves
the engineers.
No window emptier
than starting over.

Dreaming, we try it ourselves:
at dark of moon we try our own
ascension, come back in a grieving
guise, ticket our memories.

And we look to our journeying stars
to connect or disjoin us . . .
Einstein encountered them almost
as an equal; but he left us,
our scars wheeling in water.

There were other observers:
John Donne writing a letter to
Galileo whom he believed;
the English looking at Newton
with their eyes like eggs;
Chagall, some decade,
creating a universe
out of nothing but color.

Now the moon is at full again,
and whose the power?
Old Myth, profound us.

Some earliest Orpheus
not withstanding, we are all
longing to enter the dark
through a luminous door.

Blind Date

Rock booms out
over twisting, cobbled streets.
Merry-makers, glass in hand,
surge aimlessly about.
Beaming barkers
cajole the throngs.
Outdoor dancers
writhe to a frantic beat.
Indoor comics
squeeze slow laughter
from a show-me crowd.
Then just at eleven
she comes tapping,
weaving through indifferent swarms,
this mid-life lady dressed in satin
making her nightly wake-up call.
Drinking in the sounds around her.
Nodding to the torrid tempos.
Tapping, tapping, never stopping.
Reveling in noisy pleasures,
poetry to eager ears.
Cursing the curfew
when it comes.

Surprises

For my mother, Sylvia Anna Fremer Nicosia

Sitting on the brick wall
Home of tiny spiders with their fraying webs
We sit together in the sunshine
My mother, 84, and I,
One of the few things we can still do together
Besides eat.
My mother holds her cane in both hands
And says,
"They give you good food here—
You don't get any ill effects from it
It doesn't make you throw up—
That's important."
She's found a theme she likes
And for about 10 minutes she talks
About the benefit of eating food
That doesn't give you "ill effects."
I should be bored
But I'm glad when she's found something
To be happy about—
A lot of times she just sits thinking
Or staring into space
With eyes that see not much more
Than general shapes and colors
And once in a while she says something like,
"I've lost everything . . . I have nothing left"
And then she usually feels enough for me
To add, "I don't mean *you*."
But today she comes out with something
So profound it astonishes me
That her brain with half the wiring gone
And half the neuro-chips destroyed
Can realize the plight of human life
In so few words:
"I always thought old age would be nice,"
She says, "but it's not—
I was mistaken."

Living on the Earthquake Fault

It zig-zagged
Under my house, across the back of my garden
And into the hill. The tunnel to San Francisco
Cried tears out of the middle of the earth.
And I was the one who tried to hold it together. I grabbed like a clutching
                                    grandmother,
Bridged the earth-slip with my spine.

When they said, let go, I said
I'm holding the world shut all by myself, soon
It will mend like a slit in an orange.

It takes time to learn the logic of chaos.
The open fissure
Ground up pebbles green as the coast of Ireland
Or streaked with blue like the bay; it spat out
Pieces of colored fire. My house sagged and squeaked. I went to look at the view.
                            It was
Extraordinary.

A vast new country, scarves of dark-brown water,
It waited for me; it wanted my books and my children's mother;
It needed its name, and only I could say it.

"Grief in the Evening, Joy in the Morning."

Yesterday, on the road away from town,
Knocking On Heaven's Door Mountain
lifted out of winter, drugging me
with April-green. But such beauty
can sharpen despair. That night,
at the campground, I talked to
my sister on the telephone, faraway.
She'd hit another low. My heart falters
almost daily. It runs in the family.

But morning was bright again, reliable.
Even when the car broke on my way
to the ocean, I just sat down right there
at the edge of the Estero. Washed up
amid the sea-wrack at my feet were
two dead birds—no substance, no body,
just nests of feathers, one brown, one white,
returned to the Grand Abstract.

It takes awhile to tear loose from town,
to float free, driftwood among uncertainty.
I was just beginning to break away,
this second day out, hoping for glimpses.
Again the day saved, calling "Stay and
look," at that Egret's impeccable white tux,
its snake neck cocked to stab with javelin head,
that comes up, a wiggling fish hooked
on the tip, about every third try. How adroitly
and precariously, each of us survives.

I haven't learned yet to rest well
in all the long dreary stretches between.
The nondescript road slowly climbing
from the Estero I exercised numbly.
But I fly up each time, at unexpected
thresholds. That rise, over which sudden
Pacific appeared, breeze drumming
a gallant windbreak of great Eucalyptus,
as if the surf transformed at the shore

(continued)

into waves swaying inland across the fields.
That's when I noticed the glinting sea-bottom
had been waiting there all along, lifted up
in the green landscapes around me.

Cowpies laughed, splattered upon this road
to the coastguard rescue station, where
radio towers blinked, and listened for emergencies,
to save or lose lives. Oh sister, memories can't
warm up my heart enough either when it's dark, but
looking back from where I'd come, the sight
of a pearl-white road, singing alongside the Estero,
ground-up shells laid down on the oyster-farm lane—
that simple earth magic returning again, and again

JOYCE LIVINGSTON

Three Ways of Seeing Wild Mountain Trillium

1
Eight nuns on slender stalks
proud and plumed in white wimples
beyond reach on the high bank.

2
Eight bat rays rise and spread
their green wings in the sea.
Graceful limbs undulate on a current of air.

3
Spent star heads centered on broad leaves
glide in triangular formation but for one
outsider who makes a constellation.

Evening Poem

for Carolyn Kizer

Enlightenment should come easily
noting the absence of wind.

But it's a measuring worm
on an ivy leaf
that attracts attention.

The yellow cat has gone to see the white cat.
Petals of four kinds of camellia
fall gracefully into sadness

And there is nothing to improve
the extravagant silence.

Flowing through silk sleeves
are all memories of previous things.

And the pine tree beyond the garden
is seen again
to be a resting place

For birds
who come no nearer.

Sea Experience

We were drawn by blue skies
and a rock band at Land's End
to try the bridge
but when we turned
a fog brought zero visibility
and it was too late
to think twice.
We ran in circles
but could not stay forever
near the flashing buoy
for ships move in the night.
We listened for the wind
we could not see
the tide
seemed omni-directional,
the fog horns
conversing across the channel
seemed safe
until we spun and
heading straight for land
heard horns on either side.
There, compassless
gazing at the spinning tide
under a lost sky
we listened with all our senses
(whoever thought of lifejackets
was a traitor to us all).
We were an organism
all intelligence, all experience
all our senses played.
Then the red lights of the bridge
and we emerged
knowing only that we had acted
with all our senses
and had by accident
arrived.

11.

The name of a person ("X") to whom letters have been written a function of the subject composed on a page, these "facts" including the way one chooses a path down the cliff to the beach, the rope (fixed) meaning to counteract gravity, the shape of the approaching wave as it builds (sequence), shifts and eventually breaks. How the person's image may be reproduced as an image that cannot be inferred from those events, the one whose hair (washed) is covered with a towel emerging from the bath in that sense the cause rather than effect of emotion. Why as the tape begins to play words take on a kind of momentum interior to what is being spoken, the bird disappearing from the branch whose resultant motion may be thought to echo this or that series of ascending notes.

◆ *Grapes*

bunches of them
        fields of them
sagging the vines

I remember driving
        dozens of wooden stakes
into recalcitrant soil

I remember
        palms blistering open
and the insolent midday sun

16 ounce bottles of orange Fanta
        sourdough
           and provolone

the sweating
        spitting
    swearing

for this

        blood ripe
   and glistening.

Makins

"Makins" they said,
"all rolled into a tight child
ready to be lit."
"Lots a good kindling" they said,
"leaning jest right.
You're like wet wood" they said
"have to smolder awhile
to get those sparks going.
When the wind of lovin starts,
WATCH OUT.
Life is comin' round!"

Why Animals Dance

Because of their clickety hoofs
Because of their scritchety claws
Because of their crackety beaks
Because they don't have any boots

They shiver their milliony feathers
They leap with their backlegs together
The fish dance the top of the water
and mean to be dancing forever

They look to the white dancing master
The disk that spins faster and faster
till her edges spin off and powder the earth
and the breeze and the trees with her laughter

They dance through the hole in the night
They dance to the back of the light
who's hunting around on the wrong side of town
with his cage to lock them in tight

Here we are! Here we are!
They cry from afar,
Come join us down by the river!
But the light moves away
into the new day
and the creatures keep dancing forever

Meeting a Lizard
on Mount Tam

Time being what
    it isn't, never
        (ever becoming)

able to boast
    unequivocally
        "Present"—I

likewise, (shouldn't
    I?) mutter my
        ambiguous

Me, *sotto voce*
    (i.e. under my
        death). Knowing

as the woods try
    fire for fashion
        how even this

Absolute Lizard—
    stunned in a sudden
        ambush of sun—

will, if you
    contemplate it,
        twitch the least

last finial
    of tongue, its
        rock-steady eye

horrendous
    jocular
        mocking.

The Red Wagon

If it weren't for the red wagon
Jean would have seen the car
left-turn the corner coming
down the street
at her kneeling
putting right the wheel come loose
straightening too the handle
angled askew from too many kids
too many years.

        The wheel
slid in easy, a
notched indent clicking solidly
onto double layers of metal placed
just so to catch it—the handle too—
eager almost—
springing into place strong and firm.

        When the car hit, the bumper tore
one wide gash under her neck
the blood spurting
into the air spilling onto the wagon—
crushed.

        The wheel rolled
all the way down the street
past the house where susan's kid ate
wheaties with milk and rested near aaron's
mother's car—the blue one—the
white top rusting from years of
neglect from the rain and the snow.
It rolled near the curb and
spun crazily.

This Evening

Held twice, how can the house be empty?
There is your body in my arms
and there is you, hovering discreetly

in memory, or field
that becomes prairie-like with you
in the green, that body which discloses you

even when you're gone.
Now you are slipping onto the blue sofa,
bringing the prairie indoors

switching the lamps, the lupine,
the low clouds solid as ceilings overhead,
it matters little either way. Matter

isn't the focus here. Here
is out of place. This is the prairie
that radiates out in circles, so that one

room may not lead to the next
and comings and goings turn time.
The slope rises to bay trees, where you are

ankle deep in a stream, or beckoning
from the porch, urging the gold salamander
into deeper water where it becomes safe.

It's evening.
The last reddish-gold of the day
catches in your palm as you wave.

The lights wander house to house. We are
on the sofa, and I am reaching toward you
with all that I can feel, and my hands.

Crop Circles

The key is grain; grain is the key.
Unlock the universe
and open up the door-less door
of passage, wherein we
unlock the universe.
Alpha is Omega. Speak no more
of passage, wherein we
recycle our phenomena.
Alpha is Omega. Speak no more.
The artisans are children who
recycle our phenomena.
Concentric circles amply ring around
the artisans. Our children who
go camping out in fields of grain,
(concentric circles, and play ring around
the rosy in the nighttime, then
go tramping out the fields of grain
in cryptic keys,) have found
the rosy. In the nighttime then
they claim an acreage here. We too,
in cryptic keys have found
a distant People. Celebrate the rights
they claim: an acreage. Here we too
will never starve again.
A distant People celebrate the rites
of passage, wherein we
will never starve again.
The key is grain; grain is the key.

Late October

Leaves float off the trees in the first good rain.
Green smells slide down mountain slopes, wake
buried bulbs, mushrooms,
tell birds to nest,
fill my young pointer's nose
with keen ache
I watch travel through his body
like melody.

An old stone lion on the library steps
yawns in slanted moonlight, tosses back slumber.
His body ripples. Tawny hair bristles,
now a curly, full-fledged mane.

Longing steps out of the shadows,
looks me in the eye. Astonished,
growling softly, I ease my way forward,
follow angled light
towards knife-clean scent.
As I imagine "yes,"
night hums back
"where?"

To Hand

Bone star
Alone we make
what could have touched
and had touch retrain
whatever vagrant shape
is a wall, whatever held up
the falling city when you
succumbed to fragility, first
your own and then how it came
to belong.
And so you belong here
where the sky doesn't
reach the ground. Cloven
hour and stone flare.
How we knew you were here to stay
among us.

Return

they bring their voices into the forest
sounds that carry the weight of promises
the pressing in of walls
loud, plaintive sounds that strain to be heard
understood
sounds that lower, slowly
with the working of muscles
letting their legs take on the effort
step by step
higher and higher into the pristine
light of afternoon

and in the walking
they give their wounds to the mountain
betrayals, abandonments
open and bleed
drop down the spine into soil
like seeds for saplings next season
they step over seeds buried by others
unknowingly blessing them with their feet
like fingers on the foreheads of newborns
they rest and drink from crude pipe fountains
breathless and exhausted

they are unrecognized ceremony
they are baptisms
and deep spruce-colored wakes
initiations
rites of passage
water and blood
they are redwoods
stillness
they are the son returned home

My Eyes and Tongue Remember
What My Heart and Mind Forget

Life escaped my father's body twelve years ago last March.
The previous Thanksgiving he came out to California
for a visit to my wife and me.

My last goodbye was at our house
before my wife returned him to the airport and
a many thousand miles of flight.

I remember one small dinner in Sonoma
and the restaurant of mirrors that reflected us
with parmagean, red wine, and cooling life.

His frailty and exhaustion marked each step and lifted fork.
We never said a word of death,
the curtain he would disappear behind.

I snapped his picture
as he sat and ate,
his silly hat protecting him from drafts I never felt.

Italian food was our last pleasure then:
Tomato sauce. Red pepper flakes the last fire he could face.
He shook them out in silent union with
his own dead dad, who needed them like salt.
Italian men united in our warm and hungry mouths:
Gerardo; Tony; Rocco; Gene,
the slowest simmer that reduced us to the West.
New York and Pittsburgh, Johnstown, San Francisco.

By steamships, airplanes, rental trucks,
we pass through distance, life, and love.
salut, and *mangia, filio mi.*

The Revelation of the Golf Cart Sutra

I am looking down the bright fairway
into a well manicured future
and a world without sand traps.

This flag pole at the fifth green
marks the former foundations of hell,
an old, dirty, red brick welfare house.

Here I sink the putt and again attain par
in the very place whores and addicts
made love, got high and collected food stamps.

I have not seen a homeless man in a year;
only caddies, millionaires and service workers
occupy the square mile I now call home.

This new driving wood cost me a whole day's
consulting and features a titanium shaft;
you know, your wardrobe is a bit dated.

See these Dockers shorts—Nordstroms.
They come in eight colors—I got 'em all.
I don't sabotage my looks or my swing.

Watch this shot—perfect lift, straight away.
It takes discipline and practice—no fudging.
Your main problem in life is your attitude.

What you need is a new set of clubs—
oh yes, and a few years of medical school
and a golf cart that really works.

Marsh hawk drops,
     and moments later rises . . .
          talons filled
               with emptiness.

Those Mornings, Big Sur

Up the canyon, when we dropped
to rest, we could hear the sea breaking,
sometimes a rush of doves.
We were splitting open old buckskin
logs, redwood butts and punkins
handloggers left by the creek
when they went for more booze,
long before a sawlog got winched out of here.
We never heard the dolphins
strangling in the drag nets, we couldn't see
the stain spreading out from the rusty stern,
the horizon turning brown.

                        Our paths cut down
through Costanoan midden, abalone shell, lupine
and granite dust. We broke an urchin
open on the slippery rock, squeezed a lemon
and sucked the sharp morning from our hands.
On a minus tide it was all there to dig
and pry from the hissing cliff, one swell after
another, before the big plate glass was tilted
up around brass fittings, before the coast
road was oiled slick as another roll of film
and tanker diesels churned the milkshake yellow.

We pumped south of Malpaso Creek for rock fish
or some bawdy wisdom before Hollywood
came and cut the old ranches up
for props. Beyond the little boat
pulling in snapper and cabazone
a barge line was stretching tight
to Japan, but we didn't see it.
Light shattered in the kelp
between our laughing and the big slick
blubber flukes rolling south
out of sight. The blown ridges plunged down
into mist, and the headlands, long and ragged
as a condor's wing, kept curving
out of sight.

We thought
the seams of the freighters were welded tight,
as we climbed up through coyote bush
to raise our kids in a blaze of redtails.
We believed we could hoist and chink the stones
Jeffers had left grinding below the ocean
drive, thought the trails to our rustic towers
would be too rough for the inspectors, too steep
for the realtors. We couldn't see
the factory ships flushing their bilges,
the old growth forests piled high
on the barge decks, north creeks running red
mud out of clearcuts and smoking craters,
our dream coast hacked and hauled off for sushi
while some country music played
in our cabins, and we believed
our muddy roads would keep out the world.

The Nursery

Rows of babies in plastic boxes,
faces red as worms freshly
brought forth from earth.
New elements in the vast disorder
swinging around them.

All the other lives
they will not lead
extinguished; labeled now,
they have been slotted
into place. Still wing-deep
in ether they push off,
constructing holograms
for others, beginnings
that brighten the rhythm
for the moment
for the rest of us
as when a crowd of cedar waxwings
making a gift of themselves,
net the tree with wild sounds,
flash their brief and beautiful greed.

They will march over meadows
hip-deep in yellow blossoms;
listen for winds from the south
to sweeten the path;
pick their ways through thickets
spangled with the breaths of panthers,
befuddled like us
by their weapons—
the faulty gestures they will brandish—
the stubborn convulsions of the heart.

They too will hear going by
what they have failed to find.
They will shelter always under
leaves splitting
the light and shadow
in patterns that cannot hold.

Lined up now like swimmers
in their lanes, eyes clenched.
Moorings cut
form the dream of zero
they are leaving, for a while.

Poet's House

Swatches of light startle
        the fine dust
                on the windowpane—

brief residue of sunlight
        below a tight canopy
                of California oak.

This house you saw
        as a house for poets:
                cedar shakes, windowseat,

slanted ceilings in the small
        upstairs rooms.
                Tree House

you said, now
        the body that absorbs
                our traits, our art:

a carpet from Isfahan
        a Japanese triptych,
                the Shona sculpture that made us cry.

I've been washing spinach,
        mixing honey-mustard
                with snips of bacon

for the special salad
        I will eat alone,
                not quite alone,

in this place we inhabit like spirits—
        you in Iowa
                and me staying where most

of my bad habits have changed
        and remain changed—stepping up
                to the ecstasy and its companions:

the washed spinach,
        the teak bowl,
                the salad tongs with antelope

carved into them,
        a single slice of purple onion
                on a white plate.

JOYCE LIVINGSTON

1 < *Pacific Rims* >

The sky don't work any more.. That's why those lines..
Them weaves of blasts—furrowing across the lower air..
Shredding hearts...oppressive weights.. disbursed thickly
Because the upper atmos are wounded beyond repair...?

Our lies never work... Hard enuf to keep score..
Losing a game so precious as this, the whole bloody...
Well, you probly don't think so.. What with ideals
& concerns, affections & duty, processing & working..

I don't beg.. Least not like ways most seem to think..
I hollar & scream inside, & shake what I can
To dance my way thru.. Holding you wd help, tho.
& being held by you.. wd dream us beyond any pale..

One nite I cryd dry tears,.. I sat meditating.. in that tent.
Where... those sweet old marshes were conquered by our war machines..
A very base thing to do—even with current recompense;..
How do you pay humans, tho we're one, for what's done to birds..?

I cdn't write or speak or vibe or talk or chat
With you then.. I felt you're going.. When there's nothing
To go to.. Tho I admired, sort of still do, your bold
Attack...In getting things done for beings...No matter..

Then I knew (Here I doubt.. & that's what made me cry,
In a fore-bemoaning moan of loss before any try is there)
Truly I saw clear how well & good & kind we'd love.
Not some therapeutic fantasy, or elegiac devotion,.. but love!

There are many fine younger poets in Marin County. These poets and their poems represent but a sampling of the poetry being produced yearly.

Some began writing on their own and some came to poetry through their schools, or through the Marin poets who work with the California Poets in the Schools program. Large numbers of high school students enter the annual poetry contests offered by the Marin Poetry Center and other organizations. Although the poems included in this section could stand on their own merit, they are grouped to highlight the fine work coming from our talented poets eighteen years and younger.

Student Self-Portrait

His hair is a hawk sitting on his head.
Hers, a sack of gold found by a pirate.
Together, their eyes are the creek by their school,
their ears, funnels catching the wind,
their noses, treacherous cliffs with small caves,
teeth like little pieces of paper, snow falling in winter . . .
Natalie's *Imagination* is a jogger running
farther than anyone can see.
Kirsty's is a thousand horses galloping.
Lily's *Fear* is a big black snake strangling her
into darkness. Lizzie's *Loneliness* is a woman
with long black hair and sad blue eyes.
Dan says *Boredom* has bulging muscles
that stretch across the land, all the way to Peru,
where Marco is reminded of his name,
someone rolling dice, calling out the numbers.
Sylvia says *Red* comes from the laughter of God
on a hot summer day. Shannon thinks *Sleep*
has blue tie-dyed hair; Micah said he once heard
the sound of warm blankets humming.
Looking up at me, from behind her glasses,
Grace says that books are a deep blue sea you enter
by opening the covers, each one with different words,
like fish swimming on a page, each one
with different meanings, like *Constantinople.*
They're like Sharon's stories that she says come out at night,
like a herd of cows, *each word a cow,* she says.
And when they walk past, her voice changes,
like all their voices change: into a southern drawl,
an autumn breeze, the silence after storms.
So many songs, all just waiting to be sung.

—Karen Benke

Compiled into a poem taken from the words of the poets in grades two and three.

Dear Mama,

As I write this
words won't agree with me
the wall of my guilt
encases myself
ideas bouncing from
an unwanted shield

Your love
is like water
an oasis
   ~ ~ ~ shimmering
among painted desert
sands
decorated by paths
   ~ ~ ~ of the wind ~ ~ ~
which is almost
the only thing crossing
and surviving

I am a fish
straining to walk
to reach you
to swim in your
cool affection
to be wanted
by you

I await
searching for strength
to evolve
to find within myself
the wings to reach you
to touch your heart

                Yours truly,
                   Hannah Jane

Invisible People

EVERY SINGLE DAY is the same as before,
begging for money and knocking on your door

I breathe the same air, I walk the same streets—
you go by car, I go by feet

I am a recluse, you are a king—
 you walk with pride, I walk unseen

When I look at you, I wish it was me—
when you look at me, there's nothing to see

> CHORUS: (Oo, Invisible People)
> Put yourself in my shoes,
> put yourself in my shoes
>
> put yourself in my shoes,
> and see how it would feel

✦

INVISIBLE PERSON PASSED on the street,
people turn from me and wish they could delete

The unseen person they will never know,
something's wrong with the way I go

Can't ask for help, too much dignity—
don't want to be viewed with your sympathy

Hours turn to days, days turn to nights—
lived like this so long, I've given up the fight

> BRIDGE:
> Take another look and see how you would see,
> if I were you and you were me

✦

(continued)

THERE'S A MAN walking down a New York street,
he has no job and he wants to eat

He has to follow all the rules,
he doesn't want to be just another fool

Last in his class, he couldn't enhance,
he really wanted that one last chance

He doesn't want to fade away,
he wants to be part of the everyday way

◆

I FOUGHT ALL year in the war for you,
there wasn't really anything I could do

I was drafted against my will,
I was sent to Vietnam to bomb and kill

Thousands died, few were recognized,
our efforts were never realized

We all had kids and a wife we barely met,
one in three homeless is a Vietnam vet

Lyrics and music by the Class of 1998, seventh graders, at Marin Country Day School.

The Death of Six Million

The stench of old, well-worn leather
[muddy shoes]
fills the room
[piles and piles—hundreds]
I feel nauseous & cover my nose
[some small enough for children]
a lady cries
[some large enough for a grandfather]
her husband reaches out and grasps her hand
[next to the shoes, piles of spectacles]
still, tears drip slowly down his cheeks too
[starved, tortured to death]
never again, never again
[or maybe some had to give up]
"THERE ISN'T ANY MORE ROOM FOR HATE"
[wouldn't you?]
a wise, wise man once said
[after witnessing the slaughter of your innocent friends]
and as he said it, his eyes filled with pain
[the world is cruelly twisted]
as if all the suffering in the world
[horribly unfair and unjust]
sat solely on his broad shoulders
[because people will not accept differences]
if only there were more like him
[and millions of names blew into the sky with the ashes]

Sunlight Breaks, Papermill Creek

Reflections

The wild wind gusts
Again and again
Then stops
And a splash of color catches my eye
As it is whisked through the air

The leaf lands at my feet
And I bend over to pick it up
Its stem is hard, like the shell of a tortoise
A thin green stripe is printed down its middle
Suggesting the time that it spent swimming in the breeze
On the outstretched arm of a tree

Beyond the green
The leaf is tickled with yellow
Orange, red, and brown
Telling me that the lifetime of this leaf
Is ending

As I finish studying
Each perfect spot
And each slender curve
The wind gusts again
And the leaf jumps from my hand

It leaps into the air
And glides towards the river
And is carried away
Like my mind in a dream
A dream of summer and spring, of fire, of death

The leaf escapes the wind, and falls to the ground
I remember where I am
I forget the leaf
I forget the river
I forget the dreams

We Remember

I still remember buttons on a shirt,
eraser dust, the sound of people walking,
a running sink, the softness of a pillow.

I remember the shrimp and the tacos,
the brown color of the people,
the whistle in the streets, my ring
and my girlfriend leaving.

I can remember the clap in church,
the sound of the staff's keys, the taste
of zucchini, buttered walnuts,
fried spaghetti eggs. I loved the smell
of your upper lip.

I remember a flute and ice-cold lemonade,
a candy apple red Mercedes with gold dayton rims,
the smell of marijuana and apple pie, the sound
of a huge wave breaking.

I can hear gunshots and screams—smell of smoke.

The touch of a baby's skin,
the touch of the tip of a pin,
a room hot boxed by weed.

Raindrops and wind, sour lime, salt.

I remember the taste of wheat grass
in the morning, red in the eyes of fire,
that which is pure after a rain.
The smell of the sea. I still remember
a girl's perfume, the music of water,
bandana-blue.

Compiled by Molly Fisk from lines by Ruben, Jared, Juan, Jesus, N'Kosi, Jose, Oscar,
Joe, Cosmo, Iman and four anonymous.

Crimson Tide

Stepping into the enclosure
I breathe fresh air, while
the outside smoke gathers
like a cloak, drawn tight
against the evening air,
smothering life like a deadly pillow.

In the distance a hue of orange
and bright scarlet surges
across the sky as the flickering flames
dance to and fro.

Acres of land barren, burnt of life,
still stand, and tremble,
as the wind whips
through the defenseless stumps.
The sting of the lash pushes
the great flames onward

Bits and pieces of ash adrift
on the wandering breeze take flight,
and soar—
remnants of the flood

The Poets

Etel Adnan is an American poet and writer born and raised in Lebanon. She taught Philosophy at Dominican College in San Rafael, is an internationally exhibiting painter and tapestry-designer. Her works include *Journey to Mount Tamalpais, The Indian never had a horse, Paris, when it's naked, Of cities and women* all published by The Post-Apollo Press. (Sausalito)

Ellery Akers is a writer, artist and naturalist. She teaches at the Bay Area Women Poets Workshop. *Every Day* first appeared in *Barnabe Mountain Review.* (Inverness)

Karla Andersdatter, poet, novelist, storyteller and teacher lives and works at Muir Beach. A native Californian, she claims genetic heritage as a 'mongrel' with ancestors from all corners of the country, and a heritage mixture from many countries. She holds a Master's from UCLA. *Strawberry Fields* is from her book *The Broken String* published by Plain View Press. (Sausalito)

Lea Aschikenas graduated from college in 1995. She moved to Costa Rica for 8 months covering Central American politics for a newsmagazine. She freelances with *The Pacific Sun* and *The San Francisco Bay Guardian.* She has had poetry published in *The (Baltimore) City Paper, The San Francisco Bay Guardian, Albatross* and *The Maryland Poetry Review.* Her poem, "Looking for Home" was written when she was twenty, and teaching English at the Canal Ministry in San Rafael. (Mill Valley)

Joan Baranow, a native of Ohio, has a Ph.D. from Rutgers University, has won awards from the Academy of American Poets and in 1992 received an Individual Artists Fellowship from the Ohio Arts Council. Her poems have appeared in *The Antioch Review, The Western Humanities Review, The Spoon River Poetry Review* and elsewhere. (Mill Valley)

Evelyn Belvin An old banana / a bag of licorice / an *arrangement* of old purple flowers / now dried and brittle, / an oil lamp without oil / a bottle of saki / neglected – / another arrangement / of old dried remnants / from a bouquet – / a glass of pens & pencils; / to the right, on the wall / wonderful photographs / cartoons with meaning and, / a tiny, old, glamorous snapshot of me – it is on the salt cellar. (Tiburon)

Karen Benke teaches in the *California Poets in the Schools* program. Her writing has been included in the anthologies *Where the Heart Is: A Celebration of Home* and *An Intricate Weave: Women on Girls and Girlhood.* "Coming Home" received first place for the 1995 *David Ross Memorial Poetry Award.* She lives in a small cabin by a creek. (Mill Valley)

Duane BigEagle is an American Indian of the Osage Tribe. He has a B.A. from the University of California at Berkeley and has been writing and publishing poetry for 25 years. He has been teaching in the *California Poets in the Schools* program for twenty years. He has received three Arts in Residence grants from the California Arts Council, is a Lecturer in American Indian Studies at San Francisco State University, was a 1992 Artist in Residence at the Headlands Center for the Arts, and recipient of the 1993 Gerbode Poetry Award. He is a traditional Southern Straight Dancer and a member of the Blue Horse Singers, a Native American drum group. (Tomales)

William Binzen is a fine art photographer as well as a poet. He won the Bay Guardian Poetry Contest in 1993, BACA Juror's First Award 1991, Juror's Award, Falkirk Cultural Center 1990 and received a Marin Arts Council Grant in Photography, 1990. He has photographed and directed art projects in the Black Rock Desert, and has six book-length photography portfolios, among other projects. (Woodacre)

Claire Blotter is a writer, performer and director who has taught at universities and colleges throughout the Bay Area and now teaches writing workshops privately. She received a Marin Arts Council Grant in Poetry and has two poetry books, *Trying to Sing in the War Zone* (1990) and *Face* (1996). She has twice won SF Performance Poetry Slam titles and competed nationally. She has received major grants in theater and video. She has recently had poems in *A Summer Room* and *convolvulus*, both Marin publications. (Sausalito)

Katherine Bonenti has lived in Marin for twenty five years. Her work has been published by *The Advocate, Anderie Poetry Press, Mill Valley Literary Review, the Commuter Times* and this summer will be included in an anthology, *The 33 Review.* (Larkspur)

Barbara Brauer is a freelance writer and editor with more than 20 years experience in the publishing field. A board member of the Marin Poetry Center, she is co-author, with Jackie Kirk, of *The Face of AIDS:* (San Geronimo)

Margaret Butterfield works as an editorial assistant to Simone Fattal at The Post-Apollo Press in Sausalito. She is a contributor to *Rooms,* has a limited edition broadside *A Snarl Unlike,* and *Everything is Real Except the Obvious* from Em Press, 1992. (Lagunitas)

Patricia Cannon has lived in Marin for 18 years. She currently works in child care for a family in San Anselmo, while she studies to be a pediatric nurse. She has been published in Volume One and Volume Two of *The 33 Review.* (San Rafael)

Mary Castelli is the recipient of the 1994 Clark College poetry award, and her work has appeared in *Iowa Woman, Ruah, Broken Bridges, Rio Grande Review, Riversedge* and others. She has a chapbook called *Shape of a Song*. (San Anselmo)

David Castleman After we moved to Mill Valley from British Columbia, my father bought a tiny lumberyard, which recently celebrated its centennial. When I was 8 I began to work for the yard as a laborer, watched a man cut his hand off on the saw when I was 11. We had many famous customers, such as Alan Watts and Sterling Hayden who would sit beside the office counter and pour vast amounts of scotch-laden coffee into their bellies, and Benny Bufano, who sculpted that defiantly laconic image of a bear which guards the fire station in Ross. *Portraits and Stores*, 1996. (San Geronimo)

Claudia Chapline's poetry, art and photography have been published by *Noetic Science Review, Corondel, La Buhardilla, convolvulus, Estero* among others. She has two chapbooks, *Perimeters*, and newly *Egret*. *Adama Street* is a collection of poetry from San Miguel de Allende, both in English and Spanish. Her paintings and sculptures have been exhibited thoughout the U.S. and internationally. She was one of the foremost innovators in Southern California art during the 1970s. (Stinson Beach)

Nancy Cherry is co-editor of *Fish Dance*. Her poetry has appeared in *Poetry Flash, Seattle Review, Kansas Quarterly, Sou'wester, Estero, Green Fuse* and many others. She was nominated for a Pushcart Prize and for the *Best American Poetry*. She was awarded Honorable Mention and a residency at Villa Montalvo, as well as awards and grants. She has three chapbooks, most recently *Gardening in the Deep-End* from Radiolarian Press. (Fairfax)

Catharine Clark-Sayles practices internal medicine and geriatrics in Mill Valley. She has had poems published in *The Western Journal of Medicine, Writing for Our Lives*, and *Poets on Parnassus*. She is well endowed with cats. (San Rafael)

Gillian Conoley teaches at Sonoma State University and is founder and editor of *Volt*. Her collections of poetry include *Beckon, Tall Stranger* (nominated for the National Book Critics' Circle Award), *Some Gangster Pain*, and *Woman Speaking Inside Film Noir*. She received a Pushcart Prize in 1994, and received awards and fellowships from the Academy of American Poets, The Washington Council of the Arts, and the Coordinating Council of Literary Magazines and Small Presses. Poems have appeared in *The American Poetry Review, New American Writing, Poetry, American Letters and Commentary*, and others. (Corte Madera)

Ruth Daigon is editor of *Poets On:*. She has won "The Eve of St. Agnes Award" (*Negative Capability*) 1993, and was runner-up in 1994. Her latest poetry collection is *Between One Future and the Next*, Papier-Mâché Press, 1995. In her previous life as a singer, she sang at Dylan Thomas' funeral and collaborated with W.H. Auden on a recording of Elizabethan verse and song for Columbia Records. (Mill Valley)

Greg Darms was born on the Berkeley-Oakland line, went to school in Napa, school in Davis and school in Bellingham, Washington. He moved to Western Canada and planted trees and learned how to teach. Which he did for quite a while before moving to West Marin. He still teaches, edits the literary quarterly *convolvulus* and the monthly poetry calendar and newsletter *Fish Dance*. Poems have appeared in *Tight, Barnabe Mountain Review, Bellowing Ark, Poets on:, Lucid Stone* and *Limestone*. (Inverness)

Dolores de Leon has been a flamenco dancer both in this country and in Spain. She has been a choreographer (Oakland Ballet), Dance Director, teacher and a dancer of Classical Ballet, Modern Dance and Jazz. All this she brings to her poetry and to her book in progress *Gypsy Flamenco*. (San Rafael)

Albert Flynn DeSilver is a visual artist as well as poet, and likes to combine the media. He has a BFA from the University of Colorado, and an MFA from the San Francisco Art Institute. He is the author of two collections of poetry: *Another Right Angle Dismantled,* and *Olive Juice,* and he has a third work in progress. (Woodacre)

Kathy Evans teaches poetry at Juvenile Hall and through The California Poets-in-the-Schools. She is the author of *Imagination Comes to Breakfast,* and poems have recently appeared in *The Alaska Quarterly, The Pacific Review, Sow's Ear,* and *Yellow Silk.* She lives on a houseboat with her daughter. (Sausalito)

Ella Eytan has been a social worker and an antique dealer. Now she is a poet and will remain a poet. She is Co-Chair of the Marin Poetry Center. She has been published in *Poet Lore, Seattle Review, Loonfeather, Bay Guardian* and others. (Mill Valley)

Jody Farrell After a primary career as mother of seven and a late-life career as director of a mental health agency, she is retired and involved in the Music Festival, the AIDS Fund, KSAFE (an older women's group), and Seven West Marin Writers. "Ruins" was written during the time of her son's illness and death from AIDs. It is one of a collection of twenty poems on the subject which she hopes to publish this year as *Orion Rising*. (Point Reyes Station)

Molly Fisk is the poetry editor for the West Marin Quarterly, *Estero.* She teaches poetry at Marin County's Juvenile Hall and with California Poets in the Schools. Her manuscript *Listening to Winter* was a Walt Whitman finalist in 1995 and a National Poetry Series finalist in 1996. Her profile of Marin writer Anne Lamott was the cover story in the September 1996 issue of *Poets & Writers Magazine.* (Stinson Beach)

Gerald Fleming edits the literary annual *Barnabe Mountain Review.* His poetry and prose have appeared in many magazines, *New Letters, Indiana Review, Poets On:, VOLT, convolvulus* and *Five Fingers Review* among them. He has taught for twenty-five years in the San Francisco public schools. His book for teachers on the writing process appeared from Allyn & Bacon in 1991. (Lagunitas)

CB Follett is the editor of this anthology. She received a Poetry Grant from the Marin Arts Council in 1995, was nominated twice for a Pushcart Prize and has two collections of poetry from Hot Pepper Press: *The Latitudes of Their Going* and *Gathering the Mountains.* She has won various awards and "Bull Kelp" appeared in *Confluence,* was winner of the Portland Poetry Contest 1994, Honorable Mention, Wildwood Poetry Prize 1995, and #3 of the WindRoom series from Radiolarian Press 1996. (Sausalito)

Christi Payne Fryday works in publishing, currently free-lancing as a compositor and designer of books, including this anthology. She has recently completed a B.A. in English Literature with a writing emphasis at Dominican College. (It's taken me a total of 27 years, and I am very proud.) (San Rafael)

Terri Glass is coordinator for California Poets in the Schools. She has been recipient of a Marin Arts Council Grant to teach poetry at the Kentfield Rehab Center and the Center for Attitudinal Healing. She has published one chapbook, *Mermaid Secret* and one book of poetry, *Unveiling the Mystical Light.* She has been published in *Calendar Magazine of San Francisco, Rigorous, Oxygen No. 6, Science of Mind, Sierra Nevada College Review, convolvulus* and other journals. About her poem, she says that Pixie Lane is a tiny switchback of a road in Homestead Valley, and a very magical place. (Greenbrae)

Dale Going is a poet and book artist publishing letterpress chapbooks of innovative poetry by women under the Em Press imprint. Her first collection of poetry, *As/Of the Whole,* won the San Francisco State University Poetry Chapbook Competition, and her second collection *The View They Arrange,* was nominated for the Poets' Prize. She received the Diane Wood Middlebrook Fellowship from the Djerassi Resident Artists Program and the Seattle Bumbershoot Award for letterpress book design. (Mill Valley)

Linda Gregg is fifth generation West Marin. She grew up in San Geronimo Valley. She and her twin sister, Louise, went to Sir Francis Drake High School. She has traveled to many foreign lands, but her home is still in Forest Knolls. She has published four books, *Too Bright to See, The Sacraments of Desire* and *Chosen by the Lion* all from Graywolf Press, and *Alma* from Random House. She has been awarded a Guggenheim Fellowship, a Whiting Award, an NEA grant, a number of Pushcart Prizes, and other honors. In 1997 she will be teaching at Columbia in the spring and the University of California-Berkeley in the fall. (Forest Knolls)

Robert Hass is the author of many books, some of which are *The Field, Human Wishes, Praise, Sun Under Wood*. He grew up in San Rafael, attended St. Mary's College and Stanford University. Currently, he teaches English at U.C. Berkeley and serves as Poet Laureate of the United States. He spends as much time in Inverness as he can. (Inverness)

Marie Henry's work has appeared in *Yellow Silk, Alcatraz, California Oranges, Bite to Eat Place Poetry at the 33 Review, convolvulus, Exquisite Corpse* and *Full Court* (a basketball anthology). (San Rafael)

Brenda Hillman is Associate Professor at St. Mary's College, has been Visiting Lecturer at several others, and been a faculty member at many Writers' Conferences. She has received two Pushcart Prizes, a Guggenheim Foundation Fellowship, NEA Fellowship, and many other awards. In 1993 she was a finalist for The Pulitzer Prize. Books include *Bright Existence, Death Tractates, Fortress, White Dress,* and *The Poetry of Emily Dickinson.* Poems have appeared in *American Poetry Review, Iowa Review, Mademoiselle, The New Yorker, Paris Review, Partisan Review, Ploughshares,* and many others, as well as anthologies. (Inverness)

Jane Hirshfield's most recent book, *The October Palace* received the Poetry Center Book Award, the Commonwealth Club of California's Poetry Medal, and the Bay Area Book Reviewers Award. Other books include *Of Gravity & Angels, Alaya.* Forthcoming are: *The Lives of the Heart* and *Nine Gates: Essays on Poetry.* She has edited and co- translated *Women in Praise of the Sacred: 43 Centuries of Spiritual Poetry by Women, The Ink Dark Moon: Love Poems by Komachi & Shikubu, Women of the Ancient Court of Japan.* She has received a Guggenheim Fellowship, Columbia University's Translation Center Award, a Rockefeller Foundation Bellagio Fellowship and a Pushcart Prize. Her work has appeared in *The New Yorker, The Atlantic, The Nation, The American Poetry Review, The Paris Review, Poetry* and numerous anthologies. She has been Visiting Associate Professor in Creative Writing at U.C. Berkeley and teaches in the University of San Francisco's Masters in Writing Program. (Mill Valley)

Sandra Hoben's work has appeared in *Antioch Review, Partisan Review, Ironwood, Quarterly West, The Prose Poem, Alaska Quarterly Review* and *Sonoma Review*, whose 1995 poetry prize she won. She has one chapbook of poetry out and is currently offering a workshop to teachers on poetry in the elementary classroom. (Mill Valley)

Sarah Howard is descended on her father's side from the Adams family and the Dukes of Norfolk, yes, those related to Catherine Howard, 5th wife of Henry VIII, beheaded—and on her mother's side from a family of Russian Jews, mostly unknown since most were massacred in pogroms. (Inverness)

Hannah Husband is thirteen years old, a poet and artist. She started writing poetry at age five working with Kathy Evans who continues to be a valued mentor. In 1993, she won Second Honorable Mention (in the 7–11 age group) in the all-Bay Area "City of Poets" Event. She is published in their anthology, as well as the *Mill Valley Literary Review.* Her short stories have placed in the Marin County Fair; and her poetry has been displayed in the traveling art show of the Children's Circle Center School as well as in *Fast Forward* a children's newspaper. "Dear Mama" was written when she was 11. (San Rafael)

Jaime Jacinto was born in the Philippines and grew up in San Francisco. He is currently on the faculty of the College of Education at San Francisco State University, where he teaches reading and composition classes in the University's Step to College Program.(Fairfax)

Marjorie Kent Jacobs lived in Bolinas for 25 years and now lives in San Rafael. She is one of the editors of *Side Show*, an annual anthology of the short story. Among other entertaining jobs, she was employed by the Marshall Plan in Paris, and the House of Representatives in Washington, D.C. She now devotes her time to writing poems. She is 79. (San Rafael)

Robin Jacobson is a consultant to writers, publishers, arts organizations and other non-profits. She is a graduate of the Eastman School of Music, trained at the Boston Gestalt Institute and is a certified practitioner of the Rugenfeld Synergy Method. She develops and leads program in the creative process. She has had poems published in *Poets On:, Barnabe Mountain Review, convolvulus, Fish Dance* and other journals. She is currently an Affiliate Artist of the Headlands Center for the Arts. (San Anselmo)

Amy Kashiwabara was born in Korea, raised in New Jersey. A recent graduate of U.C. Berkeley, she won the Academy of American Poets 1994 Poetry Competition there. She has studied with Thom Gunn and Lyn

Heijinian and has two books of poetry, *Bug* and *Pocket Meteors* from Cyborg Productions. Poems have appeared in *convolvulus, The Berkeley Poetry Review, Talking Raven Quarterly, Seventeen,* and various anthologies. (Corte Madera)

Margaret Kaufman has an MFA from the Warren Wilson Program for Writers. She leads writing workshops, serves as poetry editor for *The Western Journal of Medicine,* has served as poetry coordinator for the Napa Valley Writers' Conference and co-edits fiction for *The Marlboro Review.* She has received a Marin County Artist Grant. Her books include *Aunt Sallie's Lament, Sarah's Sacrifice, Girasole, Praise Basted In.* She has been in many publications and has two books waiting in the wings: *Snake at the Wrist* (poetry) and *Life Saving Lessons* (a collection of linked stories). (Kentfield)

Matthew Kramer spent his youth climbing mulberry trees in Ohio and lighting bonfires in San Antonio. He earned a Master's in Colorado, fell in love, and followed his favorite person to California where he lives in a houseboat and works brewing beer in the City. (Sausalito)

Joanne Kyger, native Californian, attended the University of California at Santa Barbara, then moved to North Beach in San Francisco. She has published fourteen books of poetry and her poems have appeared in numerous anthologies and literary magazines. She has taught at the New College of California in San Francisco, and in the poetics program at Naropa Institute in Boulder, Colorado. For the past twenty years she has lived in Bolinas.

Jacqueline Kudler's poems have appeared most recently in *Estero, Earth's Daughters, Poets On:,* and *Barnabe Mountain Review.* She co-writes a regular outdoors column for the *Pacific Sun,* and published a hiking book, *Walking From Inn to Inn* (East Woods Press) in 1986. She has taught writing and literature at College of Marin for the past ten years. (Sausalito)

Peter Kunz has appeared in *Barnabe Mountain Review, convolvulus, Poetry at the 33, Steelhead Special, Yellow Silk,* and in *700 Kisses.* He has been a fellow at Dorland Mountain Art Colony, The Hambidge Center, and The Millay Colony. (Inverness)

S. E. La Moure, poet, teacher, and gardener, lives in Tomales

Denise Liddell Lawson writes and lives in San Rafael, with intermittent excursions to Vermont and Morocco. (San Rafael)

Joyce Livingston is a painter and poet. She has a view of the bay, and the ocean is nearby—all of which encourages poetry to surface. (Inverness)

Richard Lloyd is a 1950's high school drop-out. He says he has no other claim to fame. (Woodacre)

Diane Lutovich is a partner in a training and consulting firm. She started writing poetry because the form was closer to the way she saw, experienced, and responded to phenomena—both internal and external. She has work published in *Barnabe Mountain Review, Atlantic Review, Lilith, Seattle Review* and others. (Mill Valley)

Robin Heerens Lysne is a writer and artist with a healing practice. Her first book, *Dancing Up the Moon, a Woman's Guide to Creating Traditions that Bring Sacredness to Daily Life* appeared in 1995 from Conari Press. She has taught poetry and holds workshops and lectures on various themes. Her work has been in *Korone, Wounded Healers,* and *Recovering Magazine,* and she has received grants from the Flow Fund, and Friends of Creation Spirituality. (San Anselmo)

Barbara McDonald has been teacher, college administrator, editor and writer. She travels, enjoys hiking, kayaking and yoga. Her work has appeared in *North American Review, Passager, The Time of Our Lives,* and *Fish Dance.* She lives by the Corte Madera Creek. (Greenbrae)

Cameron Curtis McKinley is a freelance writer/photographer specializing in travel and garden feature articles. Her work has been anthologized in several books. Her poems have been selected for 2nd place in a contest sponsored by A Clean Well-Lighted Place for Books, and runner up in the 1995 Randall Jarrell Poetry Prize. (Ross)

Joseph Millar lives with his son Daniel, aged eleven, and works as a telephone installer foreman. His work has appeared in *Manoa, Steelhead Special, Jacaranda, DoubleTake* and *Mudfish.* He won the Montalvo Biennial Poetry Competition and was awarded a grant from the Marin Arts Council. He serves on the board of directors of the Marin Poetry Center where he coordinates the Marin High School Poetry Competition. (Mill Valley)

Rosalie Moore is a third generation Californian of pioneers in the Gold Rush. She won an essay contest in 6th grade and decided (permanently!) to be a writer. She has a Master's in English from U.C. Berkeley, is a founding member of the Activist Poetry Movement, won the Yale Younger Poets contest in 1939 with her first book, *Grasshopper's Man.* She then published *Year of the Children* and *Singles & Doubles.* Her most recent book is *Gutenberg in Strasbourg.* She has also written children's stories with her husband, Bill Brown. Her poem "Astrolabe" was nominated for a Pushcart Prize. (Novato)

Bill Morrisey has lived in Marin for forty-one years. He has worked in advertising and is a marketing communications consultant. He is Membership and Open Reading chairs for the Marin Poetry Center. Bill has one book, *Body Comedy,* and a poem appeared in *Barnabe Mountain Review* recently. (Ross)

Gerald Nicosia is a poet, fiction writer, playwright and historian. *Memory Babe,* a biography of Jack Kerouac, earned him the Distinguished Young Writer Award from the National Society of Arts and Letters. He is currently at work on *Home to War: A History of the Vietnam Veterans' Movement.* (Corte Madera)

Diana O'Hehir is the author of two novels: *I Wish This War Were Over* and *The Bride Who Ran Away* as well as three books of poems: *Summoned, The Power to Change Geography,* and *Home Free.* She teaches English and Creative Writing at Mills College where she has been Head of both the Dramatic Arts Department and the English Department. She has received a number of prizes and awards, including the Devins Award for a first book of poems, the Poetry Society of America's award for a work-in-progress, an NEA award in Fiction and a Guggenheim Award in Fiction. In 1985 her novel *I Wish This War Were Over* was runner-up for the Pulitzer Prize. (Bolinas)

Burr Overstreet grew up in Nicasio in West Marin where he built, fenced, gardened, kept the springs filling the water tank, even ran a few horses and cattle and roamed the hills with his dog. Writing wasn't an early interest. Rather, sitting at the back of the class and waiting for the bell to ring. (Fairfax).

Caitlin Patler is a sophomore attending Tam High, involved in varsity water polo and swim team, basketball, piano, a job, and schoolwork At 14, a visit to the Holocaust Memorial Museum in Washington, D.C. so moved her that she sat in the lobby and wrote this poem. It has won first prize in both the 1996 Marin County High School Poetry Contest and the 1996 County Fair High School Poetry Contest, and fourth prize in the 1996 Iliad Literary Awards. It has been published in the *Marin Independent Journal* and *Other Voices.* She hopes her words will inspire others to learn about the past so tragedies like the Holocaust will never happen again. (Mill Valley)

Lynn Payton raised five kids, taught for ten years and is now in business with her husband. She was President of the Marin Poetry Center Board for three years. She lived for many years in San Anselmo in an oak forest and has recently moved to a home set on the marshland of Gallinas Creek, a place where the land meets the sky. (San Rafael)

Robert Peterson was born in 1924 and grew up in an hotel in San Francisco. In 1967 he received one of the first NEA grants. In 1972-73 he had an Amy Lowell Traveling Fellowship. *Leaving Taos* was a selection in the National Poetry Series. (Fairfax)

Danika Pramik-Holdaway moved to Marin about ten years ago—after twenty nine days of fog according to her mother. She has played, attended school, swum, run the beaches, hiked, studied and written poetry. In 1995 she attended the NGO Forum in Huairou, China, and says, "Women write poetry and sing everywhere." She wrote "Reflections" when she was 13. She attends University High School in San Francisco. (San Rafael)

Jean Pumphrey is a poet, Professor of English, and Co-Chairman of the Marin Poetry Center. She has had poems published in *ManRoot, Meadowlark, Buttons, Café Solo, Poetry Fair, Silken Cord/A Hand of Wind, Blue Unicorn*, and *Sunbury* along with work in many anthologies. She has two books: *Sheltered at the Edge*, a book of poetry, and *Poetry: The Way Through Language.* (Sausalito)

Stephen Ratcliffe teaches at Mills College and is the publisher of *Avenue B Books.* Recent books include *Sculpture, Present Tense, Spaces in the light said to be where one / comes from* and *Selected Letters.* (Bolinas)

Stefano Resta grew up in Bolinas, has a degree from U.C. Berkeley and has been around the world a few times. He has had work published in *Estero, The Berkeley Poetry Review, The Little Magazine, The San Francisco Bay Guardian* and others. (Sausalito)

Bambi Fullerton Rhodes B.A., U.C Berkeley; Apprenticeship, Bauhaus; Graduate Studies, Scripps; Life Teaching Credential, Elementary School, California. Also: TWA Hostess; Crew, boats in the West Indies; Crew, 110 foot Schooner, *Albatross*, Panama to SFO; Crew, Salmon boat, 2 years, SE Oregon; Europe, 6 months; Teacher, 25 years. (Larkspur)

Kay Ryan teaches basic English skills at College of Marin and sometimes San Quentin Prison. Her poems have appeared in many journals, including *The New Yorker, Atlantic, New Republic, Paris Review* and *Georgia Review.* She admits to three books of poetry: *Strangely Marked Metal; Flamingo Watching*, a finalist both for the Lamont best second book award, and the Leonore Marshall Prize for the best book of poetry for 1995, both from Copper Beech Press; and *Elephant Rocks* from Grove Press. In 1995 she received an Ingram Merrill Award. Her work appeared in *The Best American Poetry*, 1995. (Fairfax)

John Savant is Professor of English at Dominican College of San Rafael, former Chairman of the English Department, and Director of the Fall Poetry Series. His poetry has appeared in various journals: *The Southern Review, The Journal of Irish Literature, Sequoia, Trestle Creek Review* and others. In 1991 he was granted one of three State awards for excellence in the teaching of literature at the college level. (San Rafael)

David Schurr has worked as an engineer, teacher and consultant, and is currently and hopefully retired. He writes, "I spend my days birding, botanizing, reading, writing; a bit of folk dancing, volunteering, and jogging just about sums me up." (Point Reyes Station)

Kevin Shein has an MA from the writing program at SF State. He has co-edited *Trike Press,* run numerous reading series in the City, was for a time the poetry critic for the *Examiner* and taught literature at Dominican College. He's published five books of poems and has another two ready to go. He keeps to himself. (Novato)

Anne Bacon Soulé A member of both Marin Poetry Center and Marin Arts Council, she is probably the only *formalist* to win poetry contests consistently in the unstructured nineties. (San Rafael)

Linda Strauss is a gardener, hiker, and avid, amateur field botanist. She teaches with California Poets in the Schools, was Artist in Residence, Mill Valley Schools through the California Arts Council, performs with Poetry-Jazz-HipHop Celebration and is Co-Founder of the Blue Bear School of Music at Fort Mason in San Francisco. She is the author of *Safe Passage,* 1991, and *America Blues,* in progress. (Mill Valley)

Cole Swensen's latest book *Numen* was nominated for the PEN Center West Award in Poetry. Her other books include *Park, New Math,* (selected for the *National Poetry Series,*) and *It's Alive She Says.* An upcoming collection, *Noon* was awarded the New American Poetry Award. She is an active translator of contemporary French poetry. She has received grants from The Marin Arts Council, The Shifting Foundation, The Camargo Foundation, Fondation Royaumont and The University of California, where she recently completed a Ph.D. in Comparative Literature. She is currently teaching at the University of Denver. (Fairfax)

Bonnie Thomas, wanting to create a place of respect where the poetic voice can be heard, organizes poetry readings at Open Secret Books in San Rafael. She has been published in six anthologies of C.S.S. Publications, winning both second and third prizes. *Ursus Press* published her poetry with an Honorable

Mention. Poetry has appeared in *Up Against the Wall, Mother,* and *Soul Culture* among others. She is a member of the Marin Poetry Center and the Marin Arts Council. (Kentfield)

Gene Thomas-Salamando is a writer, producer and director for his own video company, *Grayfox Productions.* Among his corporate and broadcast clients, he also specializes in creating video portraits of family elders. (San Rafael)

Mel Thompson studies Western and Asian philosophy. He dabbles in performance art conceptualization, child-like color painting and amateur song-writing. He has been involved in legislative and legal issues that affect basic human rights. Of late, he has worked intensely in a form of performance art he calls "human sculpture." He takes his art "directly to the people" by putting his art pieces on himself in the form of costumes and wandering the streets of Marin, especially along crowded roadways. (Kentfield)

Christopher Thorsen is the founder of The Performance Edge, an executive mastery coaching and firm development firm. He is involved in international peace building in Cyprus and he holds a nidon (second degree black belt) in Aikido. He has taught haiku and creative writing in Bay Area schools, and has a book of poetry, *Gnarled Grasses.* (Mill Valley)

Stephan Torre From Montana and Wisconsin to Monterey to the Canadian Rockies, Stephan has been a "wood butcher" salvaging redwood logs, scratched a living from livestock and sawmills and is now mainly a teacher and writer. His most recent book, *Man Living on a Side Creek* won the Bobst Award in 1994. He received Marin Arts Council Grants in 1990 and 1994, He has won awards and Pushcart nominations. His work, widely published, depicts the sensuality and dramatic tension of male labor in raw natural environments – the conflicts that result from destroying with tool and machine what we love. (Point Reyes Station and Sausalito)

Laurel Trivelpiece has two collections of poetry, *Legless in Flight* and *Blue Holes,* plus four young adult and one adult novel. She has won two Marin Arts Council grants and been published in *Poetry, Field, Partisan Review, Connecticut Review, South Poetry Review* etc. (Corte Madera)

David Watts is Clinical Professor of Medicine at U.C. San Francisco and recent recipient of a Master's in English and Creative Writing from San Francisco State University. He has been published in *The Gettysburg Review, The Antioch Review, New Virginia Review, The Spoon River Quarterly* and *Yellow*

Silk, among others. His book *Uncoiled Waters* was a finalist in the 1991 Bluestem National First Book Competition and his chapbook, *The Heart's Inquiry,* a finalist in the William and Kingman Page Award for 1995. With his wife, Joan Baranow, he is editing *Poetry in Medicine,* based upon a course he created for medical students in which poetry is used to teach the human side of health and illness. (Mill Valley)

Lew Welch was a gifted poet, part of the group known as the "beat poets." He has been called "the poet laureate of Mount Tamalpais." His books include *The Song Mt. Tamalpais Sings,* and *Ring of Bone.* In 1971 he disappeared in the Sierra and no trace of him has so far been found.

Janie von Waldburg is sixteen and a junior at Marin Catholic. She has written over one hundred poems and been published in several non-profit magazines and newsletters. She volunteers at Halleck Creek Riding Club for the Handicapped, which serves as a source for her inspiration and personal enjoyment. She enjoys reading, writing, photography, horseback riding, philosophy and hanging out. (San Geronimo)

D E Wood After half a century of writing and living and thinking in the Bay Area, a curious thing happens—these poems, set of twelve—this being the first, written in Spring 1996 at Hamilton Homeless Shelter in Novato, where I stayed for a few months. (San Rafael)

◆ *The Artists*

Cover Art from a pastel by Joyce Livingston

Joyce Livingston has been a professional fine artist most of her adult life. She studied art in Portland, Oreogn, majored in art and architecture at the University of Oregon, attended the Pasadena School of Fine Arts and studied with many prominent artists. She has had many solo shows, taught and given workshops, is a painter, printmaker, and does mixed media works. (Inverness)

Illustrators

Donald Guravich is a graphic artist besides being a tree cutter. He teaches at Naropa Institute in Boulder, Colorado. He has lived in Bolinas for the past eighteen years.

The following poets also have illustrations in the book. (See poets' notes)

Etel Adnan
Claudia Chapine
Greg Darms
CB Follett
Joyce Livingston

Photographers

William Binzen The initial, and seminal, photograph of my career might be called an accident. It's a snapshot I made of my father in the summer of '55. My parents had divorced. I was very close to my Dad but rarely able to be with him. I was seven. And lost. The camera he gave me, a Kodak Brownie Hawkeye, was my solace and magic. In a double exposure, Dad's form—decapitated and translucent—rising from the ground. It seemed a kind of resurrection image to me. Today, despite being a professional photographer, I still pick up the Hawkeye. In the image reproduced on page 10 I was on Mt. Tamalpais, reaching for, reclaiming, an inner landscape I feared had been eroding away. (Woodacre)

Edgar Callaert is a life-long outdoorsman and camper. "There is motivation to look deeper, see things from different angles in another light." His photography has appeared in *Common Ground, Motorland, Marin Visitors* and others. (Mill Valley)

Bonnie Durrance has written, directed and produced both video and audio-visual productions for theaters in major museums across the country, such as the De Young Museum, San Francisco; the American Museum of Natural History, New York City; The U. S. Holocaust Memorial Museum, Washington, D. C.; The Heard Museum, Phoenix; Thomas Jefferson's Monticello; and the Cape Fear Museum, Wilmington, N. C. Under contract to the U. S. Holocaust Memorial Museum, she directed the Oral History Program's video-taped interviews of survivors. (Bolinas)

Marty Knapp lives at the gateway to Point Reyes National Seashore, where he has a photo studio and darkroom. His black-and-white landscape photographs of the Point Reyes area have appeared in numerous publications and his limited editions are in collections throughout the world. (Olema)

Scott Manchester, a fourth-generation Bay Area resident, has photographed throughout the world. His award-winning photography covers news, sports, and features that make the Bay Area such an exciting and wonderful place to live. His photographs have appeared in *Time, Newsweek, Rolling Stone, People,* and many newspapers. His photograph of the turkey vulures drying their wings first appeared in the *Marin Independent Journal.* (Petaluma—Yes, I know, but birds are not bothered by county lines. Ed.)

Cathy Shine has taught, exhibited, been published, worked for the movies, and won awards. She works in the tradition of documentary and portrait photographers whose focus is on the human condition. Her photographs were used for *100 Faces of Marin,* 1992, and she has had numerous exhibits including one at the United Nations for the Year of the Disabled. (Mill Valley)

E. Loren Soderberg, in his photography, is interested in an abstract approach to nature. He often explores its structure and sculptural qualities. Loren has been a professional photographer since 1985. Self taught, he is now teaching field seminars and adult education. He has a degree in Biological Science and a Master's in Marketing. His work has been shown in many galleries, on Sierra Club posters, a calendar of his photographs, and note cards. (Sausalito)

Colophon

Beside the Sleeping Maiden is set in Veljovic—designed
by Yugoslavian calligrapher, Jovica Veljović, who
also designed the cover font, Ex Ponto—and is
printed on seventy pound Fortune Matte. Printing
by Thomson-Shore in Dexter, Michigan.

SOUTH BEACH HOG ISLAND MUDDY HOLLOW LITTLE MESA INVERNESS RIDGE RED HILL TABLE HILL
WILLOW CAMP WEST POINT INN PINE MOUNTAIN LITTLE CARSON CREEK BON TEMPE LAKE WEST
PEAK LAKE LAGUNITAS BIG CARSON CREEK EAST PEAK SAMS DOGTOWN LAUREL DELL POTRERO
MEADOWS LONE PINE SPRING WHITE GATE RANCH DIAS RANCH COPPER MINE GULCH SUMMIT
HOUSE MASONS CAMP OAT HILL BIG TREES CAMP LIBERTY RANCH MAILLIARD RANCH ROSS
LANDING LOUISE A BOYD MUSUEM DISCOVERY MUSEUM PARADISE COVE CALIFORNIA POINT ST
HILARYS PRESERVE FORT BAKER ROCKY POINT AGATE BEACH BOLINAS POINT DUXBURY REEF
DOUBLE POINT REDWOOD HIGHWAY OLD DIXIE SCHOOLHOUSE MARIN ART AND GARDEN

CENTER TERRA LI | ELICAN INN MILL
VALLEY ART FESTI | RKET DOMINICAN
COLLEGE INDIAN | CKYS BEACH THE
BUCKEYE SALLY S | IIS PARK HARBOR
COVE OLD ST HI | ORSESHOE COVE
NORTH TOWER JC | PRESERVE MARIN
THEATER COMPAI | IR PARKSIDE FIVE
BROOKS DRUIDS | IS OYSTER FARM
MARCONI COVE | HUSE KEYS CREEK
BODEGA BAY CO | SIGHT & INSIGHT
TAM HIGH MISSI | ND GLENWOOD
SHELTER COVE E | LYFORD HOUSE
OUTDOOR ART CI | GALLINAS VALLEY
SANTA VENETIA I | HTS POINT REYES
LIGHT FREITAS MI | RK VICTOR JONES
PARK OLEANDEI | INS GREENBRAE
BOARDWALK SA | NATALIE COFFIN
GREENE PARK RC | OKS PETERS LAKE
BUFANOS SEAL E | I POETRY CENTER
GREENBRAE KEN | N CITIES NICASIO
GREEN POINT SA | IOE BEACH POINT
DIABLO LIGHT 67 | YALA COVE FORT
MCDOWELL EAST | ERMAN CLIMBING
CLUB COASTAL RA | IN EL MARINARO
MARINE MAMMA | DRAKES ESTERO
SCULPURED BEAC | I CATARACT FALLS
HOOKOOELCO PA | IAIN TOBY'S FEED
BARN PELICAN A | SE CAFE ARROYO
CORTE MADERA L | LARK CREEK INN
THE DANCE PALA | IK HICKS VALLEY
HALLECK CREEK I | iEL ISLAND FERRY
INDUSTRAIL LIGH | IESTE SAUSALITO
FERRY GUIDE DC | LARKSPUR FERRY
GASHOUSE COVE | RIN NATIVE PLANT
SOCIETY SAMUEL | BIN VINEGAR HILL
BALTIMORE CAN | WALKER RANCH

The Song Mt. Tamalpais Sings

This is the last place. There is nowhere else to go.

> Human movements,
>   but for a few,
> are Westerly.
> Man follows the Sun.

This is the last place. There is nowhere else to go.

> Or follows what he thinks to be the
> movement of the Sun.
> It is hard to feel it, as a rider,
> on a spinning ball.

This is the last place. There is nowhere else to go.

> Centuries and hordes of us,
> from every quarter of the earth,
> now piling up,
> and each wave going back
> to get some more.

This is the last place. There is nowhere else to go.

> "My face is the map of the Steppes,"
> she said, on this mountain, looking West.

> My blood set singing by it,
> to the old tunes,
> Irish, still,
> among these Oaks.

BAHIA WILD HORSE VALLY PACHECO VALLEY BIG ROCK RIDGE VERISSINO VALLEY WINSHIP PARK
MIRACLE MILE MANKAS SUNNY HILLS MT VISION FIRE COASTAL MIWOK MORNING SUN TRAIL
JACKS BEACH ABBOTTS LAGOON THE HUB DUTCH VALLEY SPIRIT ROCK POINT REYES NATIONAL
SEASHORE YEE TOCK CHEE PARK BLUE ROCK CAFE WEBB CREEK CCC MT TAMALPAIS STATE PARK
FERN CANYON TRAIL THE MT TAM & MUIR WOODS RAILWAY SWEDE GEORGE CREEK LEE STREET
LOCAL PETERS DAM COLIER SPRING TAVERN OF TAMALPAIS STAPLEVELT TRAIL GRAVITY CARS
OROURKES BENCH CARDIAC HILL STAR ROUTE FIVE LIME POINT KIRBY BEACH POINT BONITA
BOYLE PARK JERRY RUSSOM PARK NEIL OHAIR PARK HURRICANE GULCH FAUDE PARK TURTLE
BACK NORTH TOWER JOHN REEDS SAWMILL VISTA POINT MARIN THEATER COMPANY RARKSIDE
FIVE BROOKS AUDOBON CANYON RANCH WILLOW CAMP LITTLE CARSON CREEK INVERNESS